Botticelli's Uffizi "Adoration"

A STUDY IN PICTORIAL CONTENT

PRINCETON ESSAYS ON THE ARTS

Botticelli's Uffizi "Adoration"

A STUDY IN PICTORIAL CONTENT

Rab Hatfield

Princeton University Press

Princeton, New Jersey

Publication of this book has been aided by a grant from
the Andrew W. Mellon Foundation
This book has been composed in Linotype Janson
Illustrations by the Meriden Gravure Company,
Meriden, Connecticut
Printed in the United States of America by
Princeton University Press,
Princeton, New Jersey

LIBRARY OF CONGRESS CATALOGING
IN PUBLICATION DATA

Hatfield, Rab, 1937-
  Botticelli's Uffizi "Adoration."

  (Princeton essays on the arts, 2)
  Bibliography: p.
  Includes index.
  1. Botticelli, Sandro, 1447?-1510.
Adoration of the Magi. I. Title.
ND623.B7H36   759.5   75-33734
ISBN 0-691-03912-7
ISBN 0-691-00310-6 pbk.

To My Father

Contents

List of Illustrations

Preface

I⊤ is usually advisable to start out by putting one's best foot forward. But here I think the reader deserves an apology. The first and last of this book's four chapters should be readable enough. But what comes in between them will, I fear, require some effort. For the discussion of symbolism and portraiture often is necessarily difficult. And much as one might like to, one cannot cut corners and oversimplify if one's ultimate goal is the truth.

In matters of iconography, those interpretations are probably most elegant which are the most specific. In any case we have seen a great number of highly pointed interpretations in recent years. But the reader with any experience at all is doubtless aware of the absurdities to which this unhealthy trend has been leading. And there is a second, perhaps more pernicious, peril. For the overly pointed interpretation more often than not trivializes the work that it seeks to apostrophize; one comes away not so much with the feeling that the artist was the master of an *art* as with the impression that he was exceedingly clever at the invention of corn.

In seeking properly to interpret the symbolism of Renaissance pictures, it seems to me, one should never lose sight of the fact that some things cannot be known with certainty. As axioms in a *docta ignorantia* of modern iconographical studies the following surely have a place. (1) We can rarely—if ever—know precisely what a Renaissance painter had in mind when he did a picture. (As if, for that matter, he necessarily intended when he finished what he did when he started out.) (2) Not all the persons who looked at a Renaissance painting when it was freshly unveiled can have taken it to mean exactly the same thing. Does it therefore follow that there were some who understood the pic-

ture "right" and others who understood it "wrong"? Or does it
not instead simply follow that people perceived the meaning of
the picture in question according to their lights, and that great
works of art—then as now—are not limited to a single, narrow
meaning but offer a broad spectrum of meanings revolving around
a central core?

What is needed, then, is a method of interpretation that is
flexible enough to embrace the spectrum yet pertinent enough
to pierce to the core. This, I think, can be achieved only through
an effort to recapture the symbolic *language* of the painting under
consideration. And to do that, as the late Edgar Wind cogently
pointed out, it is necessary for us to know more than the painter
himself had to know. He was familiar with a sign's connotations;
we are not.

All of this may unfortunately lead to something of a juggling
act when it comes to putting one's results in prose. One cannot
keep a number of threads going at the same time and still write
acceptable English. One must therefore be content to circle back
repeatedly on one's tracks and make the best of the convolutions
that inevitably result.

An overlaid manner of presenting things does not, of course,
make for easy going for the reader. And it may also lead to the impression that one perceives ambiguities, double entendres, and
the like where one in fact perceives none. Botticelli, I firmly believe, imagined his Uffizi *Adoration* as a whole in which the parts
collaborate in unison. This need not mean, however, that a given
part might not perform more than a single function in the symbolic structure of the painting. On the contrary. Botticelli may
well have thought that the more functions a part might perform—the more links it might establish with its neighbors—the
greater the cohesion of the whole community of parts would
become. Botticelli's picture was painted in an age in which the
fourfold interpretation of scriptural passages was by no means
yet out of vogue. He had doubtless been exposed to those spiritual
exercises in which single Biblical episodes were viewed from a
succession of different vantage points—different "perspectives."
This for him did not necessarily imply ambiguity; more likely, it
implied the marvellous oneness of God and the harmony of God's
creation.

Like considerations apply to the chapter on the portraits. Portraiture, too, has its "language," with its signs, conventions, and
so on. It would have helped a great deal if one could have taken
a general knowledge of this language for granted. This one unfortunately could not do. Anyone familiar with the general run
of portrait discussions, and the chaotic assumptions on which they
are based, will know to his sorrow the reason why.

Although I take pride in being its author, I can hardly claim
that this book has been a one-man effort. I most likely would
never have become interested in Botticelli's *Adoration* had it not
been for a stimulating talk given by Marcia B. Hall which alerted
me to the fascinating problems the picture poses. Subsequent
discussions with her have been most fruitful; I hope she will soon
be publishing her own conclusions about the painting. I owe an
equal debt to Darrell Davisson, who, with his extraordinary
knowledge of the iconography of the Magi, was able to clarify
any number of vexatious points. To Richard Trexler, with his
profound knowledge of Florentine religion, I am indebted for
most of what I know about the religiosity of Botticelli's day. I
owe to Brenda Preyer what I regard as the key document re-
lating to Botticelli's picture: the first testament of Guasparre dal
Lama. As so often happens, it turned up one day when she was
looking for something completely different, and she was both
kind and alert enough to tell me about it when we came to talking about the painting. I should like to thank Creighton Gilbert
and E. H. Gombrich for having read an early draft of the manuscript. To their candid criticism is due whatever success I have
had here in avoiding the pitfalls of sloppy thinking. For having
read the manuscript in a later draft I am indebted to Sydney
Freedberg and the late Curtis Shell. And my most profound
thanks are due to James S. Ackerman, whom I think of as the
book's "father." With marvellous patience he followed it from
the first draft to last, offering encouragement when one would
have given up without it and being severe when severity was
called for.

The book's preparation was greatly facilitated by a Rush H.
Kress Fellowship at Villa I Tatti (The Harvard University
Center for Italian Renaissance Studies) for the academic year
1970-71.

Botticelli's Uffizi "Adoration"

A STUDY IN PICTORIAL CONTENT

Note to the Reader

A fold-out color reproduction of Sandro Botticelli's *Adoration of the Magi* in the Uffizi has been included as the last plate in the book.

Introduction

THE *Adoration of the Magi* by Sandro Botticelli now in the Uffizi (Fig. 1) was painted, probably during the early 1470s, for the altar of Guasparre dal Lama, located on the inner facade wall of the Florentine church of Santa Maria Novella.[1] The painting appears to have remained in place for slightly less than a century, first as the property of Guasparre dal Lama and his descendants and afterwards as that of the Fedini family, who acquired the rights to the altar in Santa Maria Novella not long after 1522.[2]

Around 1570 the altar passed into the possession of Don Fabio Arazzola (Alzarola), Marquis of Mondragone, a Spaniard who had served first as tutor and then as chamberlain to Duke Francesco I de' Medici.[3] Mondragone ordered the altar to be remod-

NB. References throughout the footnotes are given in short form. Full bibliographic data on all works cited are provided in the bibliography. The following abbreviations are used:

    ASF: Florence, Archivio di Stato
    BNC: Florence, Biblioteca Nazionale Centrale
    Laur.: Florence, Biblioteca Laurenziana
    Ricc.: Florence, Biblioteca Riccardiana

[1] For basic information on the painting, see Horne, *Alessandro Filipepi Commonly Called Sandro Botticelli*, pp. 38-44; and Salvini, *Tutta la pittura del Botticelli*, I, pp. 49-51. On its history, see Appendix II, 1-3; and Horne, "The Story of a Famous Botticelli."

[2] The altar still belonged to Guasparre dal Lama's descendants as of 7 August 1522 (see below, Chapter 1, note 57). According to the *Sepolcrario* of Gaetano Martini (Appendix II, 1) the Fedini, who relinquished it to Fabio Mondragone around 1570, had held it "for many years." It was definitely in the possession of the Fedini as of 1556: "Allora però érane passato il Padronato nella Famiglia de' Fedini, o per compra, o per eredità, che si fosse" (citation of a description of 1556 in Vincenzo Borghigiani, *Cronaca annalistica di S. Maria Novella*, III, p. 330 [in Orlandi, *Necrologio*, II, p. 397]).

[3] On Mondragone, see Horne, "Story," pp. 137-39. In early 1568 work was begun on his new house, designed by Bartolommeo Ammanati, which was

[3]

elled in order that it might conform with the others designed by Giorgio Vasari as part of the duke's project for the redecoration of the church.[4] The new altar would require a much larger painting, and so Botticelli's altarpiece was removed and reportedly taken to Mondragone's nearby palace.[5] But it probably did not remain there for long. In August of 1575 Mondragone betrayed Francesco I by advising King Philip II of Spain against entering into a contract with Francesco that would have been to the duke's advantage. His advice to the Spanish king was made known to Francesco by none other than Philip himself, and Mondragone was given until the end of September to leave Tuscany. His property was confiscated and the altar in Santa Maria Novella made over to Bernardo di Giovanni Vecchietti, a virtuoso of some renown. Vecchietti had the altar completed and commissioned for it an *Annunciation* by Santi di Tito, which is said to be the last painting that master completed before his death in 1603.[6]

In the dispersion of Mondragone's property Botticelli's altarpiece may already have entered the grand ducal collections. It might thus have been among the paintings taken to the villa of Poggio Imperiale after that building's reconstruction in 1622. In any case the altarpiece is known to have been there in 1796, in which year it passed from Poggio Imperiale to the Uffizi with an ascription to Domenico Ghirlandaio.[7] In 1848 Carlo Pini, on the basis of the description of the painting in Vasari's *Lives*, identified it as the Botticelli that had once been in Santa Maria Novella.[8]

A revised version of Vasari's description of the Uffizi *Adoration* occurs in the second edition of his *Lives* (1568):

At this time Sandro was commissioned to paint a small panel, with figures of three-quarters of a *braccio* each, which was

located at the Canto de' Cini, not far from Santa Maria Novella. It must have been at about this time that Mondragone acquired the altar.

[4] On the redecoration of the interior of Santa Maria Novella, see Horne, "Story," p. 138; and W. and E. Paatz, *Die Kirchen von Florenz*, III, pp. 667-747, *passim*.

[5] Fra Domenico Sandrini, *Notizie di Santa Maria Novella* (Appendix II, 2): "portandosi nel suo vicino Palazzo la tavola del Botticello."

[6] On Santi di Tito's picture, see Horne, "Story," p. 140; and Paatz, *Kirchen*, III, pp. 717, 733.

[7] Horne, "Story," p. 140.

[8] Vasari, *Vite*, Le Monnier, 1849, V, p. 116, n. 1.

placed in Santa Maria Novella between the two doors in the
principal facade of the church, to the left as one enters by
the middle door; and in it there is the *Adoration of the Magi*,
in which one sees so great a love in the first old Magus that,
in kissing the foot of our Lord and overcome with tender-
ness, he plainly shows that he has reached the end of his most
lengthy journey. And the figure of this king is the very portrait of Cosimo de' Medici il Vecchio, the most lifelike and
natural of those that are to be found in our day. The second,
who is Giuliano de' Medici, father of Pope Clement VII, is
seen with all intentness of mind most devoutly doing reverence
to that child and making over his gift to him. The third, who
is also kneeling and who appears as he adores him to render
him thanksgiving and confess him the true Messiah, is Giovanni, the son of Cosimo.[9]

Vasari gives here the fullest statement of his belief that the Magi
are portrayed as members of the family which controlled Florence during Botticelli's day, the ancestors of the dukes of Tuscany. As far as one can tell, this belief was universally shared by
Vasari's contemporaries. Hence perhaps the entry of the painting
into the grand ducal collections, which may have occurred during Vasari's lifetime.[10] The presumed presence of the Medici in
Botticelli's altarpiece has been no less a source of fascination for
observers in modern times than it was for Vasari. In fact, it has
come to be doubted only in recent years.[11] Vasari of course is
not concerned with identifications only. In describing the portraits he also undertakes to persuade his reader that the figures
of the Magi are marvels of "imitative" pictorial expression, protagonists who clearly convey the sense of the narrative.

The description then turns to a more strictly esthetic appraisal
of Botticelli's powers of characterization in the altarpiece:

Nor can one describe the beauty that Sandro showed in the
heads that are to be seen in it, which are turned in diverse
attitudes, some in full face, some in profile, some in three
quarter face, and some bending down, and in other ways as
well and with the diversities of airs of the young and old,

---

[9] Vasari, *Vite*, ed. Milanesi, 1878, III, p. 315.
[10] See above.   [11] Below, Chapter III.

with all those rare fancies that are able to make known the
perfection of his mastery; for he has distinguished among
the retinues of the three kings in such a way that one may
perceive which are the servants of the one and which of the
other.[12]

The reader is here brought to an awareness of the difficulties
which Botticelli posed himself in the disposition of the figures in
his painting. But he was able to manage them all. In both complexity of pose and differentiation among types Botticelli has
measured up to the highest standards of workmanship. And so
he has in the painting as a whole. For it is

> certainly a most admirable work, and in coloring, in drawing
> and in composition rendered so beautiful that every crafts-
> man today is amazed by it. And at that time it brought him
> so much fame, both in Florence and beyond, that Pope Sixtus
> IV, having had the chapel built in the Palace of Rome, and
> wishing to have it painted, ordered that he should become
> the head of the works.[13]

The description of the Uffizi *Adoration* is the longest of any
painting discussed in the "Life" of Botticelli. In fact the Uffizi
Adoration seems to have been Vasari's favorite Botticelli. In the
final paragraph of the "Life," in which he speaks of the diligence
and love that Botticelli put into all his paintings, Vasari comes
back to the picture as the example that makes his point. The
more interesting version of this passage occurs in the first edition
of the *Lives* (1550), in which Vasari alludes to the influence of
Savonarola's ideas upon Botticelli's art:

> Truly Sandro deserved great praise in all the pictures that
> he made, in which he was constrained by love and passion;
> and even though he may have been directed, as has been said,
> to the things by which the beautiful considerations of art
> are, through hypocrisy, rendered tiresome; it does not there-
> fore follow that his works are not beautiful and greatly

[12] Vasari-Milanesi, III, pp. 315f.
[13] *Ibid.*, p. 316.

praised, and especially the panel of the Magi in Santa Maria Novella.[14]

Vasari's description of the Uffizi *Adoration* makes it clear to one familiar with his critical biases that he regarded the painting as a work of deliberate complexity.[15] In this he was almost certainly right. But he was wrong if he thought that Botticelli had done an unusually difficult painting solely in order that he might show off his talents. For Botticelli, as I hope to show, was here dealing with subject matter demanding the greatest subtlety in figuration. The conceptual core of his picture appears to be an intricate structure in which complementary themes and several levels of meaning are conjoined. With so much stuff in its conceptual fabric, Botticelli's *Adoration* could hardly be other than complex—or else disastrous—as a painting.

But although it is complex, the Uffizi *Adoration* is by no means one of Botticelli's more abstruse compositions. For the scene in the Uffizi *Adoration* is solidly organized. Depth is not wholly sacrificed here to planar dispersion, as it often is in other of Botticelli's most ambitious works. In short, Botticelli has gathered a great deal of content into a tight and comparatively "natural" image—a concentrate of remarkable energy—and thus ap-

[14] Vasari, *Vite*, 1550, I, p. 496. The second edition has: "Meritò, dunque, Sandro gran lode in tutte le pitture che fece; nelle quali volle mettere diligenza e farle con amore; come fece la detta tavola de' Magi di Santa Maria Novella, la quale è meravigliosa" (Vasari-Milanesi, III, p. 323). Although the first to give a lengthy and evocative description of the Uffizi *Adoration*, Vasari was by no means its first admirer. It is mentioned by Francesco Albertini in 1510 (*Memoriale di molte statue et picture*, p. 14): "la tavola de' Magi, fra le porte, di Sandro Botticelli"; by Francesco Baldovinetti in the *Memoriale* he began in 1514 (where it is listed as a work of Alesso Baldovinetti's; Poggi, *I Ricordi di Alesso Baldovinetti*, pp. 49f.): "Dipinse [Alesso] una tavoletta d'altare a l'entrare in Santa Maria Novella a man ritta de' tre magi che dichono è ssì bella chosa [*in margin*: la detta tavoletta fu colorita da Sandro Botticello che visse nel tempo di Alesso e fu miglior maestro di lui]"; in the *Libro di Antonio Billi*, compiled before 1530 (ed. Frey, p. 29): "una tavola in Santa Maria Novella alla porta di mezzo"; and by the Anonimo Magliabechiano (Gaddiano), who wrote between 1537 and 1542 (*Il Codice magliabechiano*, ed. Frey, pp. 104f.; Fabriczy, "Il Codice dell'Anonimo Gaddiano," p. 84): "et [in] Santa Maria Novella dipinse una tavoletta di altare che è accanto alla porta di mezzo de' Magi che vi sono più persone ritratte al naturale."

[15] On Vasari's preferences, see Alpers, "Ekphrasis and Aesthetic Attitudes in Vasari's Lives" (further references there).

proached the kind of pictorial organization that Heinrich Wölff-
lin recognized as the leading principle of the classic style of the
High Renaissance. The precise control which Botticelli has established over the several elements of his painting must have been
what caught the eye of the somewhat academically-minded Vasari and led him to praise the Uffizi *Adoration* above all other
works by the painter. And in an earlier observer, Leonardo da
Vinci, the same quality seems to have evoked the germ of an
idea for a more rigorous but less obviously forced way in which
pictorial elements might be fused into an active yet harmonious
image.[16]

This little book is intended as an essay on pictorial content, the
purpose of which is to present Botticelli's Uffizi *Adoration* in
all its complexity. In the hope of recapturing the original content
of the painting I shall attempt here to reestablish the frames of
reference or contexts from which the Uffizi *Adoration* might
once have been perceived. The contexts in the light of which I
propose to examine the painting were physical (the painting's
relationship to its surroundings), personal (its significance for
the patron), doctrinal (the relationship of its imagery to the
tenets of medieval and Early Renaissance theology), devotional
(the way in which it reflects trends in religious sensibility), cul-
tural (its meaning within a given social situation), and artistic
(its significance as a demonstration of the painter's skill). All of
the strands of meaning it derived from these contexts—and others
as well—were incipient parts in the appreciation of the picture
of a cultivated observer of Botticelli's day. This observer, of
course, might effortlessly sense what we are forced to seek out
through the laborious process of critical analysis. The approach
taken here perforce requires separate discussions of aspects of
the painting which in the painting itself are tightly bound together. One is up against a dilemma not unlike Heisenberg's
well-known Uncertainty Principle in nuclear physics. In assuming the critical detachment necessary to know how the Uffizi
Adoration might be perceived in its original locus in place and

---

[16] See below, Chapter IV.

time, one must forego an immediate experience of the painting—
the very response by which Botticelli must have expected it to
be perceived. For this I ask the reader's patience and hope he will
realize that the complexity of what follows is at least in some
respects a reflection of the intricate structure of Botticelli's painting.

I

The Patron and His Chapel

GUASPARRE DAL LAMA (c. 1411-1481) is one of the pettiest figures ever to have crossed the pages of Florentine history. Had he not ordered the fine picture for the chapel which was to be his burial place, it is unlikely that his name would ever have emerged from the records of the past. Fortune has been kinder to Guasparre than his actions might have warranted. For, apart from having been a nobody, Guasparre was without those parts of character which his or any other age are accustomed to praise.

He was born around 1411, the son of Zanobi the barber.[1] Zanobi cannot have been overly successful at his trade. In a tax report of 1446 Guasparre states that he wants no part of his inheritance. (In fact, he seems to have accepted it.)[2]

Guasparre appears to have begun his career in the service of the Commune of Florence. In 1435, at the age of about twenty-four, he was appointed by the Commune to serve for a term of two months as constable of the fortress of Ripafratta, on the frontier between Pisa and Lucca. For some reason, however, Guasparre's salary was withheld, while for his part Guasparre did not make over to the Commune the revenues he had collected

---

[1] Tax report of Zanobi di Zanobi dal Lama (ASF, Catasto, 69 [Sta. Croce, Bue], fol. 451r). In this report, which appears to have been filed in early 1428, Guasparre's age is given as sixteen and a half. The first modern scholar to concern himself with the life of Guasparre dal Lama was Jacques Mesnil ("Quelques documents sur Botticelli," pp. 91-94).

[2] Catasto, 646 (Sto. Spirito, Scala), fol. 879r: "Zanobi di Zanobi mio padre. È morto e non ò presa né vogljo sua eredità." There is no record of Guasparre's actually having renounced his inheritance (ASF, Repudie di Eredità, 15 and 16 [1444-56]). In 1469 Guasparre in fact reported the sale of two houses which previously had belonged to his father (Catasto, 69, fol. 451r; 616 [Sta. Croce, Bue, 1442], fol. 1113r; 905 [Sto. Spirito, Scala, 1469], fol. 337r).

during his term as constable. An impasse ensued until, in 1447, the Commune had Guasparre detained at the court of the Podestà. However, he does not seem actually to have been brought to trial. Rather, a compromise was reached in which both sides in the dispute agreed to drop their claims. For Guasparre the episode seems to have been most unfortunate. In agreeing to the compromise he lost not only the stiff fines that had been assessed for his delay in consigning the revenues he had collected, but over thirty lire in back pay. And he was never, as far as we know, appointed to public office again.[3]

Apart from this episode, the first forty years or so of Guasparre's life seem to have been quite inconspicuous. All that we know of him during these years comes from the statements he submitted for the *catasto*, the chief Florentine tax or forced loan, in which he was required to declare all his investments and immovable goods. By 1446 Guasparre had taken a wife named Cosa, the daughter of Battista di Leonardo da Empoli, who was about eighteen at the time. According to Guasparre's report, she had come to him "without money";[4] in reality her dowry was two hundred florins,[5] a figure which to be sure was fairly low for the wife of a Florentine citizen. Cosa was expecting, but the child must have died shortly after. From that time on the couple appears to have remained childless. Guasparre ends his report of 1446, like others he filed, with a plea to the tax officials to

[3] For his services as constable, the Cassa del Comune owed Guasparre about 408 lire. He in turn owed for the *retentiones* made during his term and the wine gabelles he had collected. In 1447, together with the penalties assessed for his delay in consignment, the sum he owed amounted to 374 lire. The compromise that was finally reached was formulated in a *provisione* that was passed by the Councils in June 1447. In the *provvisione*, Guasparre petitioned the Signoria to allow the amount owed him by the Cassa Generale to be credited against his debts for the *retentiones* and the wine gabelles. Clearly the loser in the matter, Guasparre consented that any remainder of his credit with the Cassa Generale be cancelled, "for the utility of the Commune." (ASF, Consigli Maggiori, Provvisioni, Registri, 138, fols. 82v-83v; and Provvisioni, Protocolli, 17, fol. 187r-v [I owe the citation of these documents respectively to Richard Trexler and Brenda Preyer]. There appears to be no record of the affair in the Atti del Podestà.)

[4] Catasto, 646, fol. 879v: "Io tolsi moglie sanza danari, ed ò pianto. 2 anni non me rimaso [*sic*] nulla, né una borsa, né una chasa. Abiatemi chonpassone."

[5] Appendix 1, 1: ". . . conputatis jn dicto legato florenis aurj ducentis quos pro eius dotibus dixit habuisse et recepisse."

consider his pitiable situation. He claims that he is badly off financially and that he is unable to find anyone willing to work a small field of his.[6] In point of fact his situation cannot have been so bad, since he had just sold for four hundred florins a piece of land willed him by his mother, the sum to be divided among himself and his three sisters.[7]

The picture Guasparre gave in 1451 is not much better. When his health permitted him to work, he reported, he was an apothecary's assistant with a salary of thirty florins a year. He and Cosa were living in a house with an annual rent of only twenty-eight lire. Again the statement ends on a note of despair: "I am infirm and have no means of living."[8] Such complaints to the tax office served no useful purpose, and Guasparre knew it. They are evidence of a mental habit he shared with many others of his day.[9] Although not to be taken at face value, they do give some measure of the man's rhetorically oriented sensibility.

But it was not long before Guasparre's prospects had brightened. On 5 January 1454, for one hundred florins, he bought a house on Via della Scala, in the parish of San Paolo, a hospital just across the square from the church of Santa Maria Novella. In 1458 he reported the acquisition of the house and indicated that he was rebuilding it. Guasparre had also made some transferrals of land in the Florentine countryside and was now the owner of a slave, for which he had paid fifty florins.[10] In 1469 his house was still only "half built," and there is no more mention of the slave. All the same, Guasparre's affairs appear to have been in good order, since there is no lament in his tax report for this year.

[6] Catasto, 646, fol. 879r-v. Of the field, Guasparre says, "Follo lavorare a opere perché pichola chosa; non truovo lavoratore, e cho' mio gran danno." At this time Guasparre was renting a house for twelve florins a year.

[7] The sale was made in 1445 but reported only in 1457 (Catasto, 786 [Sto. Spirito, Scala], fol. 734r). At this time the florin was valued at about five lire.

[8] Catasto, 687 (Sto. Spirito, Scala), fol. 424r: "Se avete sentjla di piatà, abiatemj chompassionj, però vedete sono infermo e nonn ò da vjvere." Elsewhere he says, "Al presente mi truovo malato di febre e di pegio."

[9] On the laments which might be made to the tax officials, sometimes by persons who were very well off indeed, see Procacci, "L'uso dei documenti negli studi di storia dell'arte," pp. 15-19.

[10] Catasto, 786, fol. 734r-v. Guasparre declares his slave as follows: "Truovàmj una schiava ch'à nnome Chaterina; è tturchassa; chonperàla da Francesco di Michele di Feo Dinj, gonfalone Unichorno, per pregio di fiorini 50."

Indeed, he must have had a good deal of cash, for, by selling two houses that had belonged to his father and parleying some real estate, he had made the handsome sum of 556 florins.[11]

Guasparre made out the first of his known wills on 29 May 1469.[12] In it he left the income from his new house, for the completion of which he left precise instructions to his heirs, to the friars of Santa Maria Novella for the officiation of a chapel he was building in their church under the title of "The Three Magi on the Day of the Epiphany of Our Lord, Jesus Christ." Other legacies included, in the event that he were to die without children, up to seventy lire to each of seven poor girls for their dowries, and one hundred florins to a certain Francesco di Niccolò di Cocco, who may have been a distant relative.[13] As his heirs, Guasparre designated any sons who might be born; or, if there were none, any daughters; or, if no daughters either, his wife Cosa. If he were to die without any immediate family at all, his heir was to be the chapel in Santa Maria Novella.

There is every indication that Guasparre was now on the way to success. By the date on which the first of his wills was drawn up, he had become a *sensale de' cambi* (exchange broker) for the Arte del Cambio, the bankers' guild.[14] Guasparre's profession was one which at this time was arousing a great deal of resentment on the part of Florentine merchants and bankers. The brokers were thought to be engaging in activities for which they had no license and were suspected of usury and other illicit practices. And their number was growing alarmingly.[15] As a result

[11] Catasto, 905, fol. 337r-v. Guasparre's holdings in the countryside, however, were still a source of frustration: "In su detto podere ò certi boschj, e' quali non sono di questi 4 annj da ttagliare, ma volessi Iddio che ttanto mi valessino detti boschi quanto spendo a ripararmi dal maladetto fiume dela Marina. Non per tanto posso fare che ogn'anno non mi roda qualche parte del mio pocho seminato, chome manjfestamente si vede per chi passa per la strada maestra di Bologna; siché fui matto pelato . . . chon mio gran danno."

[12] Appendix I, 1.

[13] When he had served as constable of the fortress of Ripafratta, Guasparre had styled himself "Guasparre di Giovanni di Cocco" (Provvisioni, Protocolli, 17, fol. 187r).

[14] Appendix, I, 1: "presoneta [sic] artis Cambij." Guasparre's change of profession was first noted by Mesnil ("L'Influence flamande chez Domenico Ghirlandaio," p. 72, n. 2). On the *sensali*, see Doren, *Studien aus der Florentiner Wirtschaftsgeschichte*, II, p. 605.

[15] ASF, Consigli Maggiori, Provvisioni, Registri, 158, fols. 155v-157r (22 Dec. 1467); and 161, fols. 198v-199v (19 Dec. 1470).

they were placed under strict guild supervision. On 19 December 1470 a law was passed requiring that each broker be licensed annually by one of the guilds and that his license be approved by the Mercanzia, the Florentine tribunal with jurisdiction over finance and trade.[16]

However he may have arrived at it, Guasparre's position seems to have been well established. His name is at the head of the list of *sensali* licensed by the Arte del Cambio in the first year that the new regulations were in effect and in each of the three following years.[17] There are other signs that Guasparre was doing well at this time. In a notarial act of 13 February 1473 he is named as the broker for a large deal involving the conversion of Neapolitan into Florentine currency.[18] In the bankruptcy proceedings against the estate of Bono Boni, an important banker who failed during the financial crisis of 1464-65, Guasparre is named, on 16 August 1474, as one of the banker's creditors.[19]

The rewards of Guasparre's newly found dignity followed

[16] Provvisioni, Registri, 161, fols. 198v-199v. A few modifications, which however did not affect the yearly election of the *sensali*, were made in the law on 7 February 1471/72 (Provvisioni, Registri, 161, fols. 247v-248v). Further information on it is found in Mercanzia, 310 (Deliberazioni), fols. 27v-30r; and 311 (Deliberazioni), fol. 31r-v.

[17] Mercanzia, 308, fol. 29v (3 Feb. 1470/71); 310, fol. 28v (13 Feb. 1471/72); 311, fol. 32r (12 Feb. 1472/73); 313, fol. 97v (Deliberazioni, 28 Feb. 1473/74). The *sensali* are also listed in ASF, Arte del Cambio, 20 (Deliberazioni). There are no listings in the books of either the Mercanzia or the Cambio for 1474/75.

[18] ASF, Notarile Antecosimiano, v 297, Protocollo 3, fol. 142r-v. The notary was Ser Nastagio Vespucci. It may have been Ser Nastagio who introduced Botticelli to his patron. The notary for the Arte del Cambio from no later than 1462 until 1476 at the earliest (ASF, Arte del Cambio, 19, which is a volume of *deliberazioni* for the period in Ser Nastagio's hand [he died in 1482]), he must have been in frequent contact with Guasparre dal Lama. It was he that drew up the dowry agreement when Guasparre remarried in 1480 (Appendix 1, 4). From no later than 1464, Ser Nastagio was the son-in-law of Ser Baldovino Baldovini, the chief notary for Santa Maria Novella and the Compagnia di San Piero Martire (BNC, Poligrafo Gargani, 2128). Ser Nastagio and his brothers were the next-door neighbors of Botticelli. It was either he or Giorgio Antonio Vespucci who commissioned Botticelli's *St. Augustine* of 1480 in the church of Ognissanti. (On Botticelli's relations with the Vespucci, see Horne, *Botticelli*, pp. 70-75; and Brockhaus, *Forschungen über Florentiner Kunstwerke*, pp. 99-103). Giorgio Antonio is known to have been a member of the Compagnia de' Magi, for which he wrote a sermon sometime after 1482 (Hatfield, "The Compagnia de' Magi," pp. 132f., 157f.).

[19] Notarile Antecosimiano, c 181 (Ser Giovanni Carondini, 1474-82), fol. 13v.

quickly. Some time after 24 June 1468 Guasparre became a brother in the Compagnia di Gesù Pellegrino, an exclusive religious lay confraternity which convened at the monastery of Santa Maria Novella.[20] The confraternity appears to have had great political influence.[21] For the semester from 1 September 1472 to 1 March 1473, Guasparre was one of the four captains of the Compagnia di San Piero Martire.[22] Rather different from the Compagnia di Gesù Pellegrino, this confraternity was not strictly laical but functioned as one of the secular arms of Santa Maria Novella. The other captains who served during Guasparre's term included, as always, one of the theologians attached to the monastery and one of its friars. Although the Compagnia di San Piero Martire does not appear to have been selective in its membership, its two lay captains were usually drawn from the finest families connected with Santa Maria Novella.[23]

Full success might have been in store for Guasparre had his past not caught up with him. On 31 January 1476 he was tried and condemned for fraud by the consuls of the Arte del Cambio.[24] More than seventeen years before, in order to evade a debt of thirty-three lire, Guasparre had falsified the dates of a letter of credit and of an entry in one of his account books. For this (and the fact that he first tried to lie to them about it) the consuls fined him ninety florins[25]—which sum might however be reduced by one half if Guasparre paid by the end of February. The book in which the falsification had occurred was to be confiscated. In itself the penalty imposed by the consuls might not have been

[20] On Guasparre's association with the confraternity, see Mesnil, "Quelques documents," p. 93; and *idem*, "La Compagnia di Gesù Pellegrino," p. 71. In the confraternity's *Libro di memorie* (BNC, Magl., VIII, 1282) there is on fol. 103v a list of the brothers who belonged to it as of 24 June 1468. Guasparre is not among them.

[21] The list of the brothers referred to in the preceding note includes the names of members of nearly all the established families of Florence.

[22] Notarile Antecosimiano, B 399 (Ser Baldovino Baldovini), under 8 August 1472, the date of Guasparre's election to the post.

[23] There is considerable material on the confraternity in the notarial acts of Ser Baldovino Baldovini and in the records of Santa Maria Novella (ASF, Corporazioni Religiose Soppresse [hereinafter cited as Conventi Soppressi], 102). On its early history, see Meersseman, "Etudes sur les anciennes confréries dominicaines, II: Les confréries de Saint Pierre Martyr," pp. 62-66.

[24] Appendix I, 2.

[25] That is, *three times* the salary that Guasparre had received as an apothecary's assistant.

too damaging. But the condemnation seems to have marked the end of Guasparre's career. The statutes of the Arte del Cambio are quite firm with respect to fraud. Anyone known to have committed a *falsitatem* is to be expelled from the guild.[26] Although he kept the title of *sensale de' cambi* until his death,[27] our evidence indicates that Guasparre never was active as a broker again. The lists of the *sensali* approved for the Arte del Cambio on 12 February 1476 include the names of all of Guasparre's former colleagues, but not his own.[28] From this time on Guasparre is not to be found as a *sensale* in the records of the Mercanzia, in the surviving books of the Arte del Cambio, or in the acts of its notary.

Our few notices about Guasparre during the next few years suggest that he had returned to his former mediocrity. In December 1477 he won ten lire and five soldi in a litigation against a mule driver by the name of Domenico di Niccolò Gonfienti.[29] On 17 March 1478 Guasparre made out another will.[30] It, too, contains a legacy for the endowment of seven poor girls, but they are to receive only fifty lire apiece instead of the seventy allowed in the will of 1469. Another legacy makes it clear that Guasparre's life had contained other dishonest dealings than the one which had led to his expulsion from the Arte del Cambio; "for the exoneration of his conscience" he left twenty lire to a certain Taddeo de' Ugolini, who worked as a scribe for the Monte. As his heir Guasparre appointed his wife Cosa, who was then about fifty. Evidently the old man expected at this time to

[26] However, there is some ambiguity. In the revised statutes of the guild (ASF, Arte del Cambio, 5) it is stated under the rubric, "De vetando commictentes falsitatem in arte" (fol. 24r), which pertains to all members, that the consuls *must* expel any transgressor. However, in an earlier section, "De eo qui inventus fuerit in furto vel falsitate" (fol. 17r-v), which pertains to the *sensali* only, the statutes require only that the offender be fined at least fifty lire and expelled if possible. It should be noted that the fine actually levied against Guasparre was more than ten times the minimum prescribed by the statutes.

[27] Thus the record of Guasparre's burial (ASF, Arte dei Medici e Speziali, 246, fol. 54r): "Guasparre sensale riposto in Santa Maria Novella"; and the agreement made just after his death for the endowment of his chapel (Appendix 1, 6): "Guasparis Zenobij de Lama, sensalis cambiorum."

[28] ASF, Mercanzia, 316 (Deliberazioni), fol. 30v. From 1477 on, lists of the *sensali* are no longer entered in the *Deliberazioni* of the Mercanzia.

[29] Mercanzia, 318 (Deliberazioni), fol. 127v.

[30] Appendix 1, 3.

live out his days with no important changes in his condition. In 1480 Guasparre filed another tax statement.[31] Although he does not mention the fact, his house was still unfinished.[32] His modest holdings of land in the country were unproductive and being washed away by a swollen stream. And the ululations of despair are back: "I have no trade and do nothing and don't know how to do anything."[33]

Shortly afterwards the unexpected occurred. Around 13 August 1480 Cosa died.[34] Guasparre cannot have wasted much time in mourning. Within four days after her burial in Santa Maria Novella he was married again.[35] The name of the new bride was Angelica, the daughter of Leonardo di Luca Malefici. Then about thirty-two,[36] she came to Guasparre with the respectable dowry of three hundred florins[37]—a little more than Guasparre had

[31] ASF, Catasto, 992 (Sto. Spirito, Scala), fol. 401r-v.

[32] The house is described in a report filed by Guasparre's daughter Francesca in 1495 as, "Una casetta . . . non finita ancora" (ASF, Decima della Repubblica, 1 [Sto. Spirito, Scala], fol. 493r).

[33] Catasto, 992, fol. 401r-v: "Io non traficho e no' fo e non so fare nulla, e tr[o]vomi dechrepito chon pocha sanjtà. Rachomandomj a dDjo e ala vostra dischrezionj." Here the complaint is not so gratuitous. In the section of the report in which ages are listed, Guasparre gives his as seventy (elsewhere he concedes that "a few days" remain before he will have reached that age) and requests exemption from the head tax that all Florentine men paid until their seventieth birthday; to add force to the request, he includes the information that both he and his wife are in poor health: "Ghuaspare sopradetto d'annj 70, domando esenzione dalla testa; Chosa mja donna d'annj 55, cho' pocha sanità amendue." In an earlier section Guasparre reports that around 1475 he had, "chon pocha spesa," built a *gualchiera* (fulling mill), for which he was assessed nine lire a year by the Ufficio della Torre. (Although it does not figure in his report for that year, the fulling mill in fact already existed in 1469, when Guasparre made out his first will [Appendix I, 1: ". . . reliquit et legavit domine Cose, eius uxori, podere cum molendino et gualchiera . . . loco dicto 'al Palagio' . . ."]). But for lack of water it did not work, and so the Ufficio della Torre had allowed the tax to go uncollected. For that reason, Guasparre states, he might not have declared the machine to the Ufficio del Catasto. But honesty compelled him to do so, he says, commending himself once again to the goodness of the officials.

[34] Arte dei Medici e Speziali, 246, fol. 54r (under 14 Aug. 1480): "La donna di Guasparre sansale riposta in Santa Maria Novella."

[35] Appendix I, 4. In this document, in which receipt of the bride's dowry is acknowledged, she is already described as "uxor."

[36] In the tax report filed by her father in 1451, Angelica's age is given as three (ASF, Catasto, 688 [Sto. Spirito, Nicchio], fol. 480r).

[37] Appendix I, 4.

ever declared in taxable wealth.[38] Within a few months of their
marriage Angelica was pregnant. But Guasparre did not live to
see the child, a girl who was named Francesca.[39] A dying man,
he made out his last will on 21 April 1481.[40] In it there is no
mention of charitable assistance to seven poor girls, or of most
of the other pious works he had envisioned in his earlier testaments, which he now expressly revoked. The money of course
was to go to his new heir, the child about to be born. He died
around 25 April 1481.[41]

On 27 April next, in an agreement with the prior of Santa
Maria Novella, Guasparre's widow pledged immovable goods
with a value of about 227 florins to the monastery for the endowment of the chapel that Guasparre had built there.[42] According
to the statement that she made at the time, Guasparre had inad-
vertently revoked his own bequest for its endownment. But it
seems that Guasparre's revocation of his earlier legacy had been
quite deliberate, and that he in fact wanted the money to go to
his child instead.[43] He was buried in his chapel on the day after

[38] In 1458 Guasparre's *sostanze* are given as 197 florins (Catasto, 786, fol.
734v); in 1469 as 268/10/10 (Catasto, 905, fol. 337v); and in 1480 as
284/3/7, that is, the sum entered in 1469 plus the amount assessed for a
cow, a calf, twenty sheep, and five goats (Catasto, 992, fol. 401v).

[39] Francesca was not yet born on 27 April 1481, the date on which Angelica
made the agreement with the prior of Santa Maria Novella for the endowment of Guasparre's chapel (see Appendix 1, 6; and below, note 49).
Evidently his sole heir (Angelica had another daughter named Agnoletta,
but apparently not by Guasparre [see below, note 86]), Francesca was the
recipient of Guasparre's house and his land in the countryside (ASF,
Decima della Repubblica, 1, fol. 493r-v). She was the wife of a certain
Giorgio di Calvano di Ottaviano (ASF, Notarile Antecosimiano, F 236
[Ser Antonio di Niccolò Ferrini, 1517-30], fol. 232r-v).

[40] Appendix 1, 5.

[41] The only firm dates we have with respect to Guasparre's death are
those of his last will (21 April), the agreement between his widow and
the prior of Santa Maria Novella for the endowment of his chapel (27
April), and his burial (28 April).

[42] Appendix 1, 6. Angelica promised to provide the immovable goods
herself or else to have them provided by Guasparre's heir within six months.
In fact payment was not made until some forty years later (see below). The
annuity called for in the agreement, fifty lire plus three florins, that is,
eleven and a third florins, would require a principal of about 227 florins at
the rate of five percent which was normally taken for transactions of this
kind (although in practice the yield on investments might be considerably
higher).

[43] See below.

his widow and the prior of the monastery had come to terms.[44] On 5 August 1481 a handsome book with the Office of Our Lady and the Office for the Dead was presented on Guasparre's behalf to the Compagnia di Gesù Pellegrino by one of its brothers, Niccolò di Jacopo Carducci, whom Guasparre first may have met in the Arte del Cambio.[45]

These are the known facts of any importance about the life of Guasparre dal Lama. Although fragmentary by comparison with what can be known about Florentines of prominence, they are sufficient evidence on which to base speculation on three important questions: Why did Guasparre dal Lama build a chapel in Santa Maria Novella? When did he build it? What is the date of Botticelli's picture?

In the Quattrocento the word *cappella* seems to have been used rather loosely. Any arrangement in which altar and tomb were combined might be called a chapel. The chapel of Guasparre dal Lama was of the simpler kind. Located between the central and eastern doors on the inner facade wall of Santa Maria Novella, that is, just to the right as one entered the church by the main door (Vasari was mistaken on this), it was not enclosed by solid walls. In the sixteenth century it was referred to simply as an *altare*.[46] But although Guasparre's chapel might not have stood comparison with the Cappella Maggiore or the great chapels in the transept of Santa Maria Novella, it can hardly have been undignified. In fact it must have suited a man of far greater station than Guasparre. One writer who saw it in the sixteenth century says that it was "decorated all around with lovely marbles." In a somewhat later report we are told that these marbles were

[44] Arte dei Medici e Speziali, 246, fol. 62r (under 28 April 1481): "Guasparre sensale riposto in Santa Maria Novella."

[45] Mesnil, "Quelques documents," p. 93. Niccolò Carducci appears to have been the regular *provvisore* of the bankers' guild (Arte del Cambio, 20, *passim*). He was also a witness to the agreement between Angelica Malefici and the prior of Santa Maria Novella for the endowment of Guasparre's chapel (Appendix 1, 6).

[46] Thus the section of Borghigiani's *Cronaca annalistica* based on the description of 1556 (III, p. 330; in Orlandi, *Necrologio*, II, p. 397): "l'Altare dei Magi."

carved in relief.[47] They must have provided the frame for Botticelli's *Adoration*. Since Botticelli's picture is quite small for an
altarpiece (111 x 134 cm.), it follows that the surface of the
carved frame may have been unusually great. The altar, too, was
probably of marble. In, or in front of, the suppedaneum was a
tomb slab with the patron's arms (a red chevron on a field of
gold) and the inscription: s[EPULCRUM] GUASPARRIS ZENOBII DE
LAMA.[48] And surrounding all of this was an openwork iron screen,
which must have provided space for a handful of worshippers
as well.[49]

These things must have cost a great deal. The marble work
alone may have run into the hundreds of florins. Botticelli's painting, although small, is of the finely executed kind which brought
high prices. There were probably expenses for utensils and vest-
ments for the friars who were to officiate the chapel. Finally,
arrangements had to be made for its endowment.

How can the patron have paid for such a chapel? Now, Guasparre dal Lama was not a poor man. His taxable wealth, it is true,
never rose above three hundred florins. But Florentine business-
men were adept at concealing their assets from tax officials. Besides, Guasparre seems to have been prone, as Italians still are, to
keep his wealth in nontaxable forms.

But if Guasparre dal Lama was not poor, he clearly was not
rich either. Yet he constructed a chapel which must have out-
shone those of Florentines of much greater wealth. How could
he have afforded what they could not? Here personal circum-
stances must have come into play. Guasparre and his first wife
were childless. Evidently they came to give up all hope, for in

[47] Borghigiani, in Orlandi, *Necrologio*, II, p. 397; Gaetano Martini,
Sepolcrario (Appendix II, 1): "fatto di richissimi Marmi e nobilissimi
Intagli;" Fra Domenico Sandrini, *Notizie* (Appendix II, 2): "tutto dj marmj
intagliati." On the composition of the frame, see also Horne, *Botticelli*,
p. 40.

[48] The arms are illustrated in Martini's *Sepolcrario* (Ricc., 1935) on fol.
69r. The inscription is recorded by Borghigiani (in Orlandi, II, p. 397)
and Sandrini (Appendix II, 2).

[49] The openwork screen ("uno graticholato di ferro"), for which payment was still due, is mentioned in the section in which debtors and
creditors are listed in the inventory taken on 6 November 1481 of Guasparre's estate, now the possession of his daughter Francesca, who was about
two months old. (ASF, Notarile Antecosimiano, A 380 [Ser Andrea da
Terranuova], fols. 319v-323v and 328v.)

the will Guasparre left in 1478 there is not even the provision
for an eventual child to succeed him.[50] Moreover, Guasparre was
a parvenu. His father had been a nobody, and the name of Dal
Lama meant nothing. Most Florentines of means of course had
both descendants and established names. Their money went to
their children or other closest of kin (but only rarely to wives,
who had their dowries), and to the maintenance of monuments
which the family had already erected to itself. Only after these
matters were provided for might they direct their attention elsewhere. Guasparre, however, had nothing but a wife, apparently
as heirless as himself. Thus, when the opportunity presented itself, he might put everything he had into a chapel to commemorate his name.

What may always remain a mystery is how the opportunity
presented itself in the first place. Santa Maria Novella was among
the noblest of Florentine churches. Within its walls were buried
some of the Strozzi, the Alberti, the Tornaquinci, and so forth.
How was Guasparre dal Lama, a petty man by any standards,
able to join in this exalted company? It may be that he simply
happened to have been at hand, prepared to spend a large sum,
at a time when the inner facade wall of the church was in need of
embellishment. Even so, Guasparre must have had influential
friends. Perhaps he found them in the Arte del Cambio or in one
of the confraternities to which he belonged.

Guasparre dal Lama must have contracted for his chapel in or
just before 1469. In the first of his known wills, which was drawn
up on 29 May of that year, the chapel is described as being under construction.[51] Now, this will appears to be more than a
simple indication that work on Guasparre's chapel was already
under way. Rather, it is in all likelihood the basic document re-
lating to the chapel's inception and defining Guasparre's obliga-
tions to the friars of Santa Maria Novella and theirs to him—in
other words the *quid pro quo* by which the friars were able to
enhance the holdings of their monastery and Guasparre to buy

[50] Appendix I, 3.
[51] Appendix I, 1: "capelle que per dictum testatorem construitur jn
ecclesia sancte Marie Novelle."

his way into the venerable reaches of their church. The will establishes the bequest which Guasparre's widow would be made to honor, just before his burial, by the prior of the monastery.[52] And it contains features which indicate quite clearly that it was expressly drawn up as a means of providing for the chapel.

What can have prompted Guasparre dal Lama to make out his will in 1469—and to have it drawn up in Santa Maria Novella before a group of witnesses who were, without exception, friars of the monastery? His reasons cannot have been familial. Nothing had changed in Guasparre's immediate family for the last twenty years at least, and there was little likelihood that anything would in the foreseeable future. Moreover, there is little in the testament concerning family matters which would have warranted Guasparre's going to the trouble of making it. Were he to have died intestate, his wife would have been provided for all the same. And his heredity would naturally have passed to his children, if he had any, or to his wife, if he had none.

But the chapel in Santa Maria Novella would not naturally have become Guasparre's heir were he to have left neither wife nor children. It required the testament for the chapel to achieve the legal status of one of Guasparre's "next of kin." Now, for a chapel as such to be appointed a man's eventual heir is almost unheard of.[53] The extent to which Guasparre looked upon the chapel as a projection of himself thus seems clear. And it seems equally clear that, for their part, the friars of Santa Maria Novella had insisted upon firm assurances that the chapel would always be adequately provided for.

Guasparre's first will, then, was evidently drawn up—with the active participation of the friars—for the sake of his chapel and as a guarantee that it would always be properly maintained. The chapel was to be provided with an annual income of at least fifty lire (considerably more than what Guasparre had once paid to rent a house) to cover the expenses for officiation. This was to begin as soon as the new house with which the chapel was to be endowed had been finished and the rent on it assigned to the monastery, and was to consist of Masses every week (?) for

[52] See below.
[53] It is, by contrast, fairly common for churches and convents to be designated as heirs. Clearly, Guasparre's concern was for his chapel and not for the friars of Santa Maria Novella.

Guasparre's soul and a celebration on Epiphany Day comprising two Low Masses and one High Mass.[54]

In the later 1460s and early 1470s Guasparre dal Lama's financial prospects seem to have been very bright. Yet as of 1469 he had evidently suspended work on his house and given up his slave. Clearly, his resources were now being directed toward his chapel. It does not seem that work can have begun on the chapel long before Guasparre made out his first will in May of 1469. The dedicatory inscription on Alberti's additions to the facade of Santa Maria Novella is from 1470. Only as the work on the facade was drawing to completion do the friars seem to have begun to concern themselves with the embellishment of its inner wall,[55] which until then must have been quite bare.[56] Although Guasparre dal Lama's chapel may have been the first to be built there, it cannot long have remained without company. On 3 April 1470 a meeting was held at which the friars discussed plans for the construction of a chapel next to the west door. A picture of the Madonna was to be transferred from the Chiostro Verde to this new location.[57]

[54] Appendix 1, 1, pp. 116f.: ". . . . Post vero mortem dicte domine Cose . . . peraficatur [sic] domus predicta . . . et cum stia murata . . ."; "Jtem post mortem dicti testatoris . . . . cum dicto honere solvendi dictas libras quinquaginta ut supra reliquit et legavit."

[55] Among the acts of Ser Baldovino Baldovini, the chief notary for Santa Maria Novella at this time, are the minutes of a capitular meeting held by the friars in 1462 to discuss the tomb of the Cerchi, located in the earlier parts of the facade. The tomb had been destroyed during the work on Alberti's additions. The friars conceded that it was their responsibility to provide for its replacement. (ASF, Notarile Antecosimiano, B 394, fols. 79v-80r.) Presumably they were on their guard to avoid other expenses of the kind. On the facade before Alberti's intervention and his modifications to its lower storey, see Kiesow, "Die gotische Südfassade von S. Maria Novella in Florenz."

[56] Except perhaps for the fresco of the Annunciation in imitation of that in the church of the Santissima Annunziata, there are neither remains nor records of decorations antedating 1470 on the inner facade wall of the church. See Paatz, Kirchen, III, pp. 701f., 733f.

[57] Notarile Antecosimiano, B 398 (Ser Baldovino Baldovini), fols. 164r-165v: "facere et fieri facere tolli figuram et ymaginem gloriosissime Virginis Marie que est in claustro primo per quem jtur ad secundum claustrum maiorem dictj monasterij, et que est apud crucifissum dictj claustrj, pictam infra portam dictj monasterij, et illam conlocare et ponere jn quadam capella quam dictus civis construere et hedificare intendit in dicta ecclesia . . . apud portam dicte ecclesie et prope sepulcrum illorum della Luna." The Della Luna had their burial place near the southern end of the west aisle, that is, just in from the west door of the main facade of the church

It was not long before Guasparre was able to enjoy the honors attached to his new position as a patron of Santa Maria Novella. In reward, one imagines, for his generosity toward their church, the friars elected him captain of the Compagnia di San Piero Martire on 8 August 1472 for a six-month term.[58] This post he could not have held before he possessed a tomb in the church, since the *capitoli* (regulations) of the confraternity restricted eligibility for the captaincy to "those who are of the parish of, or else have their burial place in [Santa Maria Novella]—or at least are of the quarter,"[59] and Guasparre was of neither the parish nor the quarter.[60]

Until the time of his second marriage little seems to have changed in Guasparre's attitude toward his chapel, which he clearly regarded as his chief means of self-perpetuation. Probably the chapel was completed before 31 January 1476, when Guasparre's condemnation by the consuls of the Arte del Cambio put an end to his career as an exchange broker.[61] In any case its construction seems to have strained his modest resources, because he never did get around to completing his house,[62] a job which, according to the terms of his first will, would have to be finished by his heirs in order for the chapel's endowment to become effective.[63] In his second will, of 17 March 1478, Guasparre made some additions to the original endowment. At the chapel was to be held, from the year of Guasparre's death, an Anniversary Mass with Office for the Dead on each 7 January, that is, the day after the Feast of the Epiphany.[64] Each May a lamp was to be

---

(Stefano Rosselli, *Sepoltuario Fiorentino ovvero Descrizione delle Chiese . . . della Città di Firenze e suoi Contorni* [BNC, II, I, 126], [1657], II, ii, fol. 20v, no. 151). Without the consent of the Della Luna the project for the new chapel could not be authorized. The name of the prospective patron was being withheld.

[58] See above, p. 16.

[59] ASF, Conventi Soppressi, 102 (Sta. Maria Novella), 324, fol. IV: "e' quali siano del populo o vero siano di sepultura di detta chiesa—o almeno siano del quartieri."

[60] Guasparre belonged to the parish of San Paolo. Curiously, although he lived little more than a stone's throw from the church of Santa Maria Novella, he was registered in the quarter of Santo Spirito.

[61] See above, pp. 16f.

[62] Above, p. 18.

[63] Above, p. 14.

[64] Appendix I, 3, p. 122: "Jtem amore Dei . . . prout dictis fratribus, capitulo et convenctuj videbitur. . . ."

kept lighted at the altar.[65] Provision was also made, "for the love
of God and for the remedy of his soul," for Masses of St. Gregory
to be said once a year during the three years following Guasparre's death at his chapel, and once at the church of San
Marco.[66]

But with a new wife and the prospect of soon being a father,
Guasparre seems drastically to have changed his attitude towards
the chapel. By now almost a septuagenarian, he was a man with
no income save what could be earned from his modest property,
consisting of his unfinished house and a few pieces of land in the
Florentine countryside, and from the investment of his wife's
dowry and whatever funds Guasparre himself still possessed. Of
these sources of income, the house was pledged for the endowment of Guasparre's chapel, and his wife's dowry would revert to
her at his death. What, then, might Guasparre leave to the child
who would now perpetuate him besides the pieces of land in the
country and his personal possessions? His response to this
dilemma was natural if rather desperate. In his last will, of 21
April 1481, the dying man revoked all previous wills,[67] leaving
his chapel only one florin a year for an Anniversary Mass, for
which no specific date was set.[68]

On 27 April next Guasparre's widow, Angelica di Leonardo
Malefici, entered into an agreement with the prior of Santa Maria
Novella for the reendowment of the chapel.[69] The then prior,
Fra Giovanni di Carlo, chanced to be one of the friars who had
witnessed the drawing up of Guasparre's first will.[70] In the text
of the agreement there is extensive reference to a *donatio causa
mortis* that Guasparre had made "a long time ago."[71] This *donatio*

[65] *Ibid.*: ". . . . Et ultra predicta . . . mediam lagenam olei."
[66] *Ibid.*: "Jtem amore Dei . . . . missas sancti Gregorjj pro anima dictj
testatoris." Masses of St. Gregory are celebrated in sets of thirty. San
Marco was the center of devotion to the Magi in Florence (see Hatfield,
"Compagnia," *passim*).
[67] Appendix 1, 5, p. 125: ". . . . capsans, jrritans et anullans omne aliud
testamentum . . . et omnino penituisse et penitere. . . ."
[68] *Ibid.*, p. 125: "Jtem reliquit, voluit, jussit et mandavit . . . florenum
aurj et de auro largum."
[69] Appendix 1, 6.
[70] Appendix 1, 1, p. 115: ". . . . Presentibus testibus . . . magistro Johanne
Carulj. . . ."
[71] Appendix 1, 6: "quandam donationem causa mortis per ipsum Guasparrem jamdiu factam."

causa mortis was in fact the section of Guasparre's first will in which, "ex titulo et causa donationis post mortem," he had provided for the chapel's endowment.[72] His subsequent revocation of it was probably uncanonical.[73] But neither the monastery nor Guasparre's widow seems to have been disposed to go to court. In the text of their agreement Angelica states that Guasparre's revocation of his bequest for the chapel's endowment was inadvertent.[74] This, however, is almost surely a legal fiction. For if Guasparre's revocation was inadvertent, his memory must have been failing badly and he could no longer have been "sound in mind," that is, fit to dispose his last will. The revocation was all-inclusive, covering even previous wills which were specially binding and could only be rescinded by means of express mention. Guasparre indicated that he could not remember that any such will existed; but if it did, he now "had repented and did repent of it in every way."[75] His revocation of the chapel's endowment seems, then, to have been quite deliberate.

For the time being, at least, the friars of Santa Maria Novella had their way in the matter. Before Guasparre was buried in their church they were in possession of a new bequest in the form of

[72] Appendix I, I, p. 117: "Jtem post mortem dicti testatoris et dicte domine Cose . . . . dictas libras quinquaginta ut supra reliquit et legavit."

[73] Juridically the *donatio causa mortis* was a gift already made, which, however, did not actually change hands until the time of the donor's death. As such it was held to be nearly irrevocable by many jurists. Thus Guglielmus Durandus, *Speculum iuris*, II, ii, "De Instrumentorum editione," xiv, 3 (ed. Venice, 1576, II, p. 722): "quam donationem . . . promitto irrevocabiliter, nisi specialiter revocarem nominando personam donatarij, et speciem, et quantitatem donationis, quam voluero revocare." Donations to ecclesiastical institutions might be retracted only in cases in which bad faith could be proved against the recipient (Durandus, IV, iii, "De donationibus," 4-6 [IV, p. 373]). For the Florentine archbishop Antoninus the requirements seem to have been less stringent. He says that the *donatio causa mortis* is revoked, "si donans peniteat, vel si liberatus est de periculo in quo erat, vel si desinat conditio sub qua donatio facta fuit" (*Summa theologica*, III, x, 4). It was evidently by "repenting" of his gift that Guasparre was technically able to retract it without having to specify the intended recipient or the nature of the bequest (Appendix I, 5, p. 125: ". . . . etiam si talia forent . . . omnino penituisse et penitere . . ."). One greatly doubts, however, the juridical validity of the "repentance" of a charitable gift.

[74] Appendix I, 6: "et hoc processit potius ex inadvertentia quam consulte et advertenter."

[75] Appendix I, 5, p. 125: ". . . . capsans, jrritans et anullans omne aliud testamentum . . . et omnino penituisse et penitere. . . ."

a promise on the part of Angelica Malefici either to endow the
chapel herself or else to have it endowed by Guasparre's new heir.
The new agreement restored—and improved upon—the terms
not only of Guasparre's first will, of 1469,[76] of which the monastery no doubt possessed a record, but of his second will, of 1478,
as well. The chapel was to have an annual income of fifty lire
for regular officiation alone.[77] Masses were to be said at least
once on every day of the year except Maundy (Holy) Thursday, Good Friday, and Holy Saturday.[78] On Epiphany Day
there was to be a "festivity of the holy Magi," with Masses and
candles, the exact form of which was left at the discretion of the
monastery.[79] On the day of Guasparre's death (around 25 April)
or within three days thereafter,[80] an Office for the Dead was to
be said for Guasparre and the other deceased of his family.[81] The
chapel was also provided with an altar lamp, which was to be kept
lighted always.[82] At least three florins were to be spent each year
on the "festivity of the holy Magi," the Office for the Dead, and
the altar lamp.[83]

But in the long run the friars had the worst of the bargain.

[76] In the text of the agreement it is clearly implied that Angelica is ad-
hering to Guasparre's original wishes: ". . . considerans qualiter de intentione . . . librarum quinquaginta soldorum parvorum . . ." (Appendix I,
6, p. 126).

[77] Appendix I, 6, pp. 127f.: ". . . emere et seu emj facere . . . valutam
pro quolibet anno in perpetuum librarum quinquaginta soldorum parvorum
et florenorum trium aurj largorum; . . . . Jn quibus quidem festo . . .
tres florenj largi quolibet anno. . . ."

[78] *Ibid.*, p. 127: ". . . . quod dictj prior . . . Jovis, Veneris et Sabbatj
sanctj. . . ." On these three days, the "white" days of the liturgical year,
no private Masses may be said.

[79] *Ibid.*: ". . . . jtem quolibet anno . . . pro tempore existente eiusdem
convenctus. . . ."

[80] This clause apparently takes into account the eventuality that in cer-
tain years the date of Guasparre's death might fall on Maundy Thursday,
Good Friday, or Holy Saturday, during which three days Masses for the
Dead are not permitted by the Church (see above, note 78).

[81] Appendix I, 6, pp. 127f.: ". . . . jtem ad ipsum altare . . . secundum declarationem predictam. . . ."

[82] *Ibid.*: ". . . . jtem quod continuo teneantur retinere unam lampadam
accensam ad ipsum altare. . . ."

[83] *Ibid.*: ". . . . Jn quibus quidem festo . . . tres florenj largi quolibet
anno. . . ." Parts of the agreement between Angelica and the prior of
Santa Maria Novella were respected by the monastery until at least the
seventeenth century (ASF, Conventi Soppressi, 102 [Santa Maria Novella],
106 and 334, *passim*).

Although Angelica had promised payment within six months,[84] they were unable to collect during her lifetime; and it took them a litigation against her heirs in the archbishop's court to obtain, more than forty years from the date of their agreement with her,[85] a sum representing less than a third of the one that had been stipulated in it.[86] It is thus not surprising that, perhaps directly after they had finally settled with Angelica's heirs, the friars were willing to contemplate the passage of patronage rights to Guasparre dal Lama's chapel to another family.[87]

Our information about Guasparre dal Lama and his chapel makes it possible to give the probable date of Botticelli's altarpiece. Until now efforts to date the picture have rested entirely upon stylistic analysis, which in turn has been strongly colored by assumptions about the ages of the persons Botticelli is presumed to have portrayed in it. Datings run from the early 1470s to around 1480.[88]

[84] Appendix I, 6, p. 127: ". . . jdcirco, ex eius mera et libera voluntate . . . ut prefertur. . . ."

[85] ASF, Notarile Antecosimiano, A 10 (Ser Andrea dell'Abbaco), fol. 283v (29 March 1522); and F 236 (Ser Antonio di Niccolò Ferrini), fol. 232r-v (7 August 1522).

[86] Ibid. Although paid for by her daughters, the endowment was considered to have been made by Angelica (ASF, Conventi Soppressi, 102, filze 106 and 334, passim). It amounted to seventy florins, although according to the terms of the original agreement it should have been on the order of 227 (see above, note 42). The friars appear to have waited until about two years after Angelica's death and then taken their claim to the archbishop's court. In the final settlement Francesca, Guasparre's heir, paid forty florins and Agnoletta, the other of Angelica's daughters, thirty.

[87] See above, Introduction.

[88] Thus Ulmann, Sandro Botticelli, p. 61: "1478"; Horne, Botticelli, p. 42: "1477"; Venturi, Storia dell'arte italiana, VII, i, p. 606: "towards 1478"; Bode, Botticelli, p. 58: "1475-76"; Yashiro, Sandro Botticelli, I, pp. 30-33: "1478-80"; Van Marle, The Development of the Italian Schools of Painting, XII, p. 68: "shortly after 1475"; Mesnil, Botticelli, p. 40: "1476-77"; Bettini, Botticelli, p. 26: "c. 1480"; Paatz, Kirchen, III, p. 733: "c. 1475"; Salvini, Botticelli, I, p. 51: "1476-77"; Freedberg, Painting of the High Renaissance in Rome and Florence, I, p. 12; II, fig. 9: "early 1470s"; Hartt, History of Italian Renaissance Art, p. 282: "early 1470s." I accept the sequence established by Horne ("Story," p. 143) for the development of Botticelli's "Madonna" type, which runs from the Gardner Madonna of the Eucharist, of about 1472 (fig. 8), through the Mary in the Uffizi Adoration to the Venus in the Primavera, of about 1478.

Style aside, it seems clear that the picture must have been done before August 1480, at which time Guasparre's first wife died and he remarried.[89] This was the moment at which Guasparre, who until then had been childless, found himself with the prospect of gaining a descendant who might transmit his name to posterity. From this time on he seems to have lost all interest in his chapel and, faced with the necessity of providing for a new heir, can hardly have been inclined to obtain an expensive picture for it. Nor does it seem likely that Guasparre's widow, who put off the chapel's endowment throughout her whole lifetime,[90] would have incurred the expense of a picture such as Botticelli's.

Hence in all likelihood Botticelli's altarpiece was painted during the 1470s. Within that decade our evidence points toward an early date for the picture. The chapel was begun in, or just before, 1469 and was doubtless well along—perhaps even completed—when Guasparre dal Lama was elected to the captaincy of the Compagnia di San Piero Martire in August 1472.[91] One of course has no sure way of telling how long it took to build the chapel. And perhaps Botticelli's picture was not ordered until the stonework there was at an advanced stage. In any event, the latest time at which Botticelli's picture is likely to have been ordered is 31 January 1476, the day of Guasparre's condemnation, which cost him a heavy fine and his job. It is quite unlikely that he ordered the altarpiece after that date—or, for that matter, that Botticelli, who was acquainted with the notary that recorded Guasparre's trial,[92] would have agreed to paint it.

The altarpiece appears to have been in place well before 17 March 1478. This is the date of the second of Guasparre dal Lama's wills, in which the chapel, apparently finished, is called the "Capella de Magis."[93] In Quattrocento documents chapels are not always referred to by the titles by which they were consecrated. Often they are described with reference to either their location, their patrons, or a well-known devotional image within them.[94] Now, the chapel of Guasparre dal Lama does not seem to have been

[89] See above, p. 26.
[90] See above, note 42.
[91] See above, p. 25.
[92] The notary was Ser Nastagio Vespucci (see above, note 18).
[93] Appendix I, 3: "eius chappelle de Magis."
[94] Thus, in the case of Santa Maria Novella: "Cappella Maggiore," "Cappella de' Strozzi," "Cappella della Pura."

consecrated to the Magi. Strictly speaking, the Magi were not saints, even if they were commonly thought of as such. According to a section of an eighteenth-century chronicle of Santa Maria Novella based on a description of 1556, the chapel was consecrated to the Epiphany of the Lord.[95] This statement seems clearly, if naively, to be corroborated by the formula found in Guasparre's first will, where the chapel is said to be under the title of, "The Three Magi on the Day of the Epiphany of Our Lord, Jesus Christ."[96] Now the phrase, "Capella de Magis," might seem to be a simple abbreviation of the earlier formula, and this may in fact be the case with the term "Capella Magorum," which is found in the agreement of 1481 between Angelica Malefici and the prior of Santa Maria Novella. But upon closer inspection one realizes that "Capella de Magis" (literally: "Chapel of the Magi Family") is simply a mistranslation of the colloquial "Cappella de' Magi" and is thus not the chapel's title of consecration but simply the name by which it was commonly known. And that name, if we are to believe accounts from the seventeenth and eighteenth centuries, was derived from Botticelli's picture,[97] which for several reasons must have gained immediate notoriety.

Two further clues to the date of Botticelli's altarpiece are found in the painting itself. There is some likelihood that the youth with the sword at the extreme left is Giuliano de' Medici (Fig. 31). He has a haircut which Giuliano is unlikely to have worn after 1475.[98] The figure standing in the extreme right foreground of Botticelli's picture is generally believed to be the painter himself (Fig. 54). This belief is probably correct. The figure has the conventional hallmarks of the self-portrait.[99] Botticelli, if the figure in question is he, has painted himself in the

[95] Borghigiani, *Cronaca annalistica*, III, p. 330 (in Orlandi, *Sepoltuario*, II, p. 397): "l'Altare dei Magi . . . sotto il titolo della Epifania del Signore." Chapels consecrated to the Magi appear to have been quite rare in Florence during the Quattrocento (see below, Chapter IV, note 10).

[96] Appendix I, 1: ". . . sub titulo trium Magorum jn die Ephyfanie Dominj nostrj Yhesu Christi. . . ."

[97] Martini, *Sepolcrario* (Appendix II, 1): "e chiamavasi 'l'Altare de' Magi' perché era stata dipinta nell'Ancona da Sandro Botticelli Pittore eccellentissimo la Storia de' tre Magi"; Rosselli, *Sepoltuario* (Appendix II, 3): "Chiamavasi 'la Cappella de' Magi' per una bella Tavola, nella quale da Sandro Botticelli Pittor raro et eccellente era stata dipinta quella Storia."

[98] On Giuliano's identity and appearance see below, Chapter III.

[99] Below, Chapter III.

stage of early manhood. He would hardly have done so had he
been over thirty.[100] Hence the self-portrait probably was done
no later than 1475.

Botticelli's altarpiece for Guasparre dal Lama may with some
confidence be dated between, say, 1472 and 1475. Greater pre-
cision does not seem possible on the basis of our present knowledge.

[100] If Botticelli is indeed portrayed (twice) in Filippino Lippi's fresco of
the *Crucifixion of St. Peter* and the *Contest before Nero of Sts. Peter and
Paul with Simon Magus* in the Brancacci Chapel in Santa Maria del Carmine, of about 1485, he can hardly be over thirty in the altarpiece for
Guasparre dal Lama. On the putative portraits of Botticelli in Filippino's
fresco, see Meller, "La Cappella Brancacci: Problemi ritrattistici ed iconografici," pp. 282f.

II

Religious Symbolism

THE Epiphany that Florentines knew during the Quattrocento was an occurrence of the highest doctrinal significance. Three kings, guided by divine revelation, had made a hard journey from far-off lands to acknowledge the new-born Child. These kings, pagans, had recognized Christ as the Savior and humbly come to worship him, bringing gold in recognition of his kingship, frankincense to acknowledge his priesthood, and myrrh as a sign that he would die for mankind. The first of the Gentiles to have believed, they were at once founders of Christian belief and personifications of devotion.[1]

In Botticelli's altarpiece two symbolic motives are given unusual emphasis. One of these is the ceremonious presentation of the gifts, here apparently symbolizing the offering of the faithful of the Eucharist. The other is the ruined buildings, symbolizing the downfall of disbelief and the salvation of the faithful through Christ's founding of his Church. These two thoughts, closely conjoined, are here given a force and cogency which they had not possessed in earlier paintings of the Epiphany.

It may be stated at the outset that one cannot give the precise meaning of what Botticelli has represented. We do not know exactly what was on his mind—or on his patron's mind—when he painted the picture. One must be content to describe the intricate but cohesive system of doctrine and practice to which Botticelli's altarpiece appears to make reference, for that is the only net in which one may hope to catch what is intended. Per-

---

[1] On the Epiphany and its interpretation, see Kehrer, *Die heiligen drei Könige in Literatur und Kunst*, I; and Crombach, *Primitiae gentium, seu historiae ss. trium Magorum evangelicorum, et encomium.*

haps indeed there is no single "correct" interpretation of Botticelli's altarpiece. It is after all a painting and not a theological exposition. Its allusive structure may be deliberately elastic—precise in image and yet open in the scope of its meaning. Therein may even lie one of the sources of the painting's beauty.

To a Florentine observer of the 1470s, Botticelli's altarpiece must have seemed a most uncommon representation of the Epiphany. Breaking with tradition, Botticelli has placed the Madonna and Child in the center of the picture, where they are seated upon a wall that projects from the jagged corner of a ruinous building. Just behind them stands Joseph, whose elbow rests on an abrupt outcropping of rock which is vaguely reminiscent of the legendary Cave of the Nativity. The old Magus does not kiss the foot of Christ, as he does in nearly all other Tuscan paintings of the Epiphany done after about 1300 (Fig. 2).[2] Rather, he gazes upon it (no doubt either having just kissed it or else preparing to kiss it). The other Magi are not shown walking toward the Holy Family to present their gifts. Like the old Magus they kneel, as if awaiting their turns (Fig. 3). The followers of the Magi (Fig. 4), usually shown at one side of the picture only, are here broken up into two groups and posed with much greater formality than had been the rule.

In looking at Botticelli's *Adoration* one is struck by the ceremoniousness of the scene. The Magi, all in the center of the picture, kneel before the Child as if performing a liturgical action. Two of them possess scarflike veils. The old Magus uses his to hold the foot of the Child (Fig. 2). That of the young Magus, now barely visible, falls from his neck over his left forearm (Fig. 3). The central Magus does not wear such a veil, but there is a transparent veil over the gift which he either is holding in his left hand or has set upon the ground in front of Christ (Fig. 3). The bystanders who surround the main figures on either side, seemingly caught up in the hush of the moment, behave for the most part as if participants in a religious devotion (Fig. 4). If in Botticelli's altarpiece the shed and rock were to be turned into

---

[2] On this motive, see Kehrer, II, pp. 192f.; and Réau, *Iconographie de l'art chrétien*, II, ii, p. 248.

the apse of a church, the wall upon which Mary sits into an altar, and the Child into an officiating priest (and Mary and Joseph removed), the picture would make an appropriate representation of a religious Office.

The markedly liturgical flavor of Botticelli's *Adoration* immediately sets it apart from most earlier Florentine representations of the Epiphany, in which the presentation of the gifts is shown as a kind of secular procession. Botticelli, it seems, has here depicted the Epiphany as the "figure" or prototype of a specifically Eucharistic action, the sacramental oblation. The chief means by which he has done so are his careful arrangement of the main figures in the center of the picture and his artful use of motives such as the veils.[3]

In narrative paintings of the fifteenth century the motive of the veil is found chiefly in scenes of the Epiphany, and even in these its use is quite rare.[4] It is found consistently in only two groups

[3] Attention was first drawn to the veils by Virginia Chieffo. They were discussed by Marcia B. Hall in a talk given at the Frick Museum in New York during the spring of 1963. See now Hartt, *History*, p. 282.

[4] In pre-fifteenth-century art the veil appears quite frequently, almost always in order to indicate the sacredness of the object which it is used to hold. Thus in Early Christian reliefs in which Christ is represented by the *labarum*-type cross, the angels or apostles who present the wreaths of victory do so by means of a veil. In scenes of the *Traditio clavium et legis* Peter and Paul often receive the Keys and Law with hands covered by a veil thrown over one shoulder. In medieval scenes of the Crucifixion the angels who receive Christ's blood in a chalice or display the instruments of the Passion often do so by means of veils, as do the angels who hold the instruments of the Passion in scenes of the Last Judgment. An example of the motive of the veil which must have been known to Botticelli occurs in the cycle of the Legend of the True Cross painted by Agnolo Gaddi in the Cappella Maggiore of Santa Croce in Florence, probably in the early 1390s. In the last scene of the cycle the emperor Heraclius is twice shown returning the Cross to Jerusalem with veiled hands. In Botticelli's own *Entombment* at Munich the women who embrace the body of Christ do so by means of veils which are thrown over their shoulders. The veil used for the purpose of offering occurs only rarely in scenes of the Epiphany from before the fifteenth century; one is found in a psalter of about 1190 in the Badische Landesbibliothek at Karlsruhe (no. 122; ill.: Kehrer, *Drei Könige*, II, p. 150). Important examples in nonnarrative painting are the veil used by the angel to present the wheat and grapes to the Child in Botticelli's *Madonna of the Eucharist* in the Isabella Stewart Gardner Museum at Boston (Fig. 8); that of the angel who hands the Child to (or

of pictures. One is the manuscript illuminations of the Adoration by the miniaturists of the Franco-Burgundian school. Of this group four examples are known, the most famous of which is a page from the *Très Riches Heures du Duc de Berry* (Fig. 7).[5] The other group comprises three paintings by Botticelli, of which the best known is the Uffizi *Adoration*, and a few others by artists familiar with his work such as Sellaio.[6] There are some other scattered examples of the motive.[7] One of these occurs in a Florentine altarpiece attributed—probably incorrectly—to Francesco d'Antonio, perhaps of the 1440s (Fig. 5),[8] which at the very least

---

receives him from) the Virgin in a painting by a follower of Filippino Lippi (ill.: Scharf, *Filippino Lippi*, pl. 125, fig. 211); and, from a later period, the presentation or "epiphany" veil found in pictures such as Sebastiano del Piombo's *Madonna del Velo*, in which the veil is being removed in order that the Child be revealed to the spectator (a motive drawn to my attention by Janet Cox Rearick).

  [5] The other examples are in the *Breviary of the Duke of Bedford* (Paris, Bibliothèque Nationale, Lat. 17294 [ill.: Kehrer, II, p. 199]); a book of hours in the Österreichische Nationalbibliothek at Vienna (MS. 1855; the *Adoration* is a close copy of that in the *Breviary of the Duke of Bedford* [ill.: Kehrer, II, p. 198]); and the *Bedford Hours* (London, British Museum, Add. 18850). (Darrell Davisson brought these and a number of the paintings enumerated below to my attention.)

  [6] The other of Botticelli's paintings of the Epiphany in which the veil occurs are the oblong panel in the National Gallery at London (Fig. 12) and the Mellon *Adoration* in the National Gallery of Art at Washington (Fig. 60). Sellaio's picture is now in the Kress Collection at the Brooks Memorial Art Gallery in Memphis (no. 61.193). The veil is also found in an *Adoration* attributed to Perugino or Fiorenzo di Lorenzo in the Galleria Nazionale dell'Umbria at Perugia (no. 180). In Ghirlandaio's tondo in the Uffizi (Fig. 61) the old Magus holds the foot of Christ by means of the cloth on which the Child is seated. In Filippino Lippi's altarpiece in the Uffizi (Fig. 62) the young Magus in the foreground holds his gift in a veil, which, however, he does not wear around his neck.

  [7] E.g., in a fresco of 1414 in the cloister of the cathedral at Bressanone (Brixen), probably influenced by the manuscript illuminations of the Franco-Burgundian school (ill.: Kehrer, II, p. 200).

  [8] The attribution to Francesco d'Antonio is due to Berenson, *Italian Pictures of the Renaissance, Florentine School*, I, p. 63. Recently the painting has also been attributed to Mariotto di Cristofano (Baldini and Dal Poggetto, *Firenze restaura* [catalogue of the exhibition at the Fortezza da Basso, 18 March–4 June 1972], p. 42). Until the flood of November 1966 the picture seems always to have been in Santa Felicita, most recently in the sacristy (Paatz, *Kirchen*, II, pp. 68, 73; and Richa, *Notizie istoriche delle chiese fiorentine*, IX, pp. 300, 308). As of this writing it is in the restoration laboratories at the Fortezza da Basso. (Badly damaged, it was displayed, face down in a plaster cradle, in the recent exhibition; Baldini and Dal Poggetto, *Firenze restaura*, pp. 41f.)

is representative of a type of Adoration that may be regarded as the prototype of Botticelli's composition.[9]

If one inspects the motive of the veil in these paintings, one realizes its firm connection with the theme of offering. The veil is not simply an article of dress. In the *Adoration* from the *Très Riches Heures* (Fig. 7) it is used by two of the kings in approximately the way in which it is used by two of the Magi in Botticelli's altarpiece. Now, on the page from the *Très Riches Heures* which shows the *Meeting of the Magi* (Fig. 6), the same two kings have costumes identical to the ones they wear in the *Adoration*, but they do not have the veils. Hence the wearing of the veils, used for the purpose of offering, may be taken as a sign of reverence toward Christ and as an indication that the gifts are sacred.[10]

[9] Stylistically the painting seems to owe something to the example of Fra Angelico. Angelico and his followers used the centralized composition in an *Adoration* on a predella panel which is now in the Prado (ill.: Schottmüller, *Fra Angelico da Fiesole: Des Meisters Gemälde*, p. 69); a small panel at Budapest (ill.: Schottmüller, p. 211); and one of the panels from the doors of the silver chest of the church of the Santissima Annunziata, now in the San Marco Museum (ill.: Pope-Hennessy, *Fra Angelico*, pl. 129). It seems possible, if unlikely, that the altarpiece attributed to Francesco d'Antonio is based on a major composition of Angelico's which is now lost. The center of devotion toward the Magi in Florence was San Marco, of which monastery Angelico of course was the chief painter in the 1440s. At least one important painting of the Epiphany from San Marco now appears to be lost. It was the altarpiece of the Compagnia de' Magi, which had its meeting place in the monastery. In the sixteenth century the painting was preserved in the sacristy, as we are informed by a notation from a now lost collection of orations by Landino: "Nota, come la Compagnia de' Magi, oggi disfatta, era la medesima Sagrestia oggi di S. Marco, nella quale ancora vi si conserva la Tavola dell'altare, che è l'Istoria de' Magi" (Bandini, *Specimen literaturae Florentinae saeculi XV* . . . , II, p. 159, n. 4; see also Hatfield, "Compagnia," p. 139, n. 154).

[10] See above, note 4. In representations of the Epiphany produced until around 1100 the Magi often present their gifts with hands covered by the edges of their coats (Kehrer, II, *passim*; Réau, *Iconographie*, I, pp. 226f.; II, ii, p. 242). This motive is occasionally found in Florentine Quattrocento paintings, e.g., in a predella panel *Adoration* by Giovanni dal Ponte now at Brussels (pointed out to me by Darrell Davisson). The motive, evidently related to that of the veil, was a sign of homage of pre-Christian origin (Réau, II, ii, p. 242). In the well-known mosaic in the apse of San Vitale at Ravenna showing the *Offering of the Empress Theodora*, the Magi, who are represented in the embroidery of Theodora's mantle, hold their gifts with covered hands. The motive of hands covered either by veils or by the edges of the bearers' coats is common in scenes of the offering of tribute to rulers (especially in antiquity), sacred books to patrons, and so on.

Whether the veils in the *Très Riches Heures* and the other illuminations of the Franco-Burgundian school indicate as well that the gifts are of a Eucharistic nature, seems impossible to determine.[11] But in the altarpiece attributed to Francesco d'Antonio (Fig. 5) they clearly have that significance. This picture is wholly unlike other surviving altarpieces of the Epiphany from the first half of the Quattrocento.[12] More than an historical event, the visit of the Magi to Christ in acknowledgment of his divinity, it shows

[11] This question hinges upon whether or not the veils are of a specifically liturgical type. From the rather casual way in which they are draped around the figures, it seems doubtful that they are. The liturgical veil to which they correspond most closely is presently known as the humeral veil (acolyte's veil; offertory veil; sacrament veil; subdeacon's veil). This is a broad scarf, worn like a shawl over the shoulders, which is used by the subdeacon at High Mass to hold the sacred elements, and by the priest for the Exposition of the Blessed Sacrament and during theophoric processions such as that of the Corpus Christi (see especially Braun, *Die liturgischen Paramente in Gegenwart und Vergangenheit*, pp. 228-31). The humeral veil was not in general use during the fifteenth century. However, various kinds of veils and cloths for handling the Sacrament have been used since the earliest times. These include the maniple, which is worn over the left forearm (on it, see Braun, *Die liturgische Gewandung im Occident und Orient*, pp. 515-61), and coverings for the sacred vessels (Braun, *Paramente*, pp. 213-15, 217f.). Other liturgical cloths were in use which might variously be described as *fano, mappula, offertorium, sindon, sudarium*, and so on. All of these words might at times refer to a scarflike veil that was held in the hands or worn over one or both shoulders (on these cloths, see especially Braun, *Paramente*, pp. 228-31; *idem, Gewandung*, pp. 517-30; and Jungmann, *The Mass of the Roman Rite: Its Origins and Development* [*Missarum Sollemnia*], trans. Brunner, *passim*). In the rite of Milan the subdeacons wore the *continentia*, a veil that hangs around the neck, when carrying the sacred vessels (King, *Liturgies of the Primatial Sees*, p. 423). In the early rite of Rome the acolytes who served at Communion wore scarves over their shoulders (Jungmann, ii, pp. 303f.). On the use by the people of veils or cloths for the presentation of their offerings, see below.

[12] On its eventual source in Fra Angelico, see above, note 9. In two of Angelico's paintings, the fresco in the Cell of Cosimo at San Marco and a panel now in the San Marco Museum, the Epiphany is coupled with an image of the Man of Sorrows, the object of the Eucharistic sacrifice (see Nilgen, "The Epiphany and the Eucharist," p. 313). The altarpiece attributed to Francesco d'Antonio may have been commissioned by Giovannozzo Pitti, a political associate of the Medici whose birthday was on Epiphany Day (*Libro secondo dell'età* [ASF, Tratte, 443*bis*], under Sto. Spirito, Nicchio, "G"). It originally was located in one of the chapels in Santa Felicita, to which chapel one of the Pitti had rights of patronage (Paatz, *Kirchen*, ii, pp. 68, 73; Richa, *Notizie*, ix, pp. 300, 308). I have not been able to discover which of the Pitti had the rights to this chapel. It is certain, however, that Giovannozzo was a patron of Santa Felicita (ASF, Conventi Soppressi, 83 [Sta. Felicita], 113, fol. 64v), whereas his more famous cousin Luca seems mainly to have patronized Santo Spirito.

a kind of *sacra conversazione*, in which is demonstrated in somewhat puerile terms the sacramental meaning of Christ's Incarnation. The Magi, their followers, and Joseph flank the iconically imagined Madonna and Child, who are seated upon an altar, directly in back of which is the manger.[13] The altar and manger are set before the Cave of the Nativity, in which are seen the ox and ass. The nature of the scene thus seems clear. The gold, frankincense, and myrrh of the Gospels have here become "figures" of the offering of the Mass, which quite literally have been offered up at the altar for sacrifice to the Incarnate Child. In this allegory of the Eucharist both the containers and the veils may be taken in a liturgical sense—the containers as pyxes or ciboriums in which the offering may be brought forward and afterwards preserved, and the veils as those articles in which it must be handled by laymen or ministers out of respect for its sanctity.[14] The Child, whose foot the young Magus touches by means of such a veil, may thus be seen under a threefold aspect. As the gifts of the Magi may signify,[15] he is at once the offering upon the altar (that mortal being whose Body is the Sacrament), the agent of its sacrifice (the priest), and its recipient (God). In short, he is shown as the essence of the Eucharist, and the Epiphany is made into the "figure" of the sacramental oblation.[16]

That Botticelli was acquainted with the altarpiece attributed

[13] Mangers in the form of altars are often found in medieval Nativity scenes. This motive is apparently of Byzantine origin. (See Schiller, *Ikonographie der christlichen Kunst*, I, *passim*.) Darrell Davisson has informed me that he believes the use of the altar in scenes of the Epiphany to be of Italian origin. Its occurrence in paintings from Germany and the Low Countries has recently been studied by Nilgen ("Epiphany," pp. 314f.). On the manger as a "figure" of the altar, see Nilgen, pp. 311f.; and below.

[14] On such veils, see also below. At High Mass it is normally the subdeacon, wearing the humeral veil (the priest does not use this veil at Mass), who brings forward the sacred elements for offering. On the subdeacon's role as the representative of the people, see De Berlendis, *De oblationibus ad altare*, pp. 115f.

[15] On the meanings which might be attached to the gifts, of which three of the most common were Christ's mortality, his priesthood, and his divinity, see Sturdevant, *The Misterio de los Reyes Magos*, pp. 80-84. According to Antoninus of Florence, citing Leo III (*Sermones*, XXXVI: "In Epiphaniae solemnitate, vi," in Migne, *Patrologia Latina*, LIV, col. 254), gold signifies Christ's regal power, frankincense his divine majesty, and myrrh his mortality (*Divi Antonini archiepiscopi Florentini . . . Chronicorum opus*, I, v, 1, 3 [Lyon, 1587, I, p. 199]).

[16] For St. Ambrose the Epiphany is the *typus* of the divine service (Crombach, *Primitiae*, pp. 751f.). On the Epiphany as a prototype of Christian devotion, see below.

to Francesco d'Antonio or another painting like it, seems clear. It seems equally clear that the veils in Botticelli's picture are meant to convey a Eucharistic meaning. In Botticelli's *Madonna of the Eucharist* in the Isabella Stewart Gardner Museum at Boston (Fig. 8) the angel who is offering to the Child makes use of something quite similar to the veils in the altarpiece to hold the wheat and grapes, which of course symbolize the bread and wine of the sacrifice. Here, too, the Child is imparting his blessing.

But Botticelli has greatly reworked the Eucharistic symbolism of the earlier altarpiece. He has made the scene more active, thus restoring to the Epiphany something of its historicity. And he is more economical in his use of images. Botticelli has done away with the obtrusive altar, relying chiefly on a careful arrangement of his main figures, the veils of two of the Magi, and the veiled ciborium just below the center of the picture to convey the sense of the Eucharist. The cave of the earlier altarpiece, with its ox and ass, has here become a rock which in this context may allude to Christ, who in his supreme sacrifice made available to mankind his body and blood—the bread and wine of the Eucharist—in order that mankind might be saved.[17] Botticelli alludes as well to the implications of the Eucharist for the worshipper. His Magi are all kneeling, possibly in reference to the receipt of Communion.[18] The cloth on which Mary is supporting Christ (Fig. 2) may well be intended as the corporal of the "altar," signifying the shroud in which Christ was wrapped after his sacrifice on Calvary (just as the myrrh the Magi are offering signifies his mortality).[19] The shed in Botticelli's altarpiece, like the one in

[17] The use of a rock to symbolize Christ is due to St. Paul's interpretation (I Corinthians 10:1-4) of Moses' drawing of the water from the rock (Exodus 17:1-7; Numbers 20:1-13): "petra autem erat Christus." The water that flowed from the rock is understood in exegesis as a prefiguration of the water and blood which came from Christ's side at his Crucifixion. Thus the Old Testament episode, in which the Israelites are saved from death by thirst, is the prefiguration of Christ's bodily sacrifice, in which, as Paul says, mankind as a whole is saved from death by spiritual thirst.

[18] In Italy it became customary to kneel for Communion during the fourteenth century (Jungmann, *Mass*, II, pp. 375f.). Lay persons, as well as ministers, were always expected to kneel before the consecrated host. As a rule, priests did not genuflect until the sixteenth century (*ibid.*, pp. 212f.).

[19] On the symbolism of the corporal, see Braun, *Paramente*, pp. 208f. Until the time of Luther the Mass was almost universally interpreted as a

the altarpiece attributed to Francesco d'Antonio, may even be taken as the canopy used to cover some altars or the Blessed Sacrament when carried in procession. And there are numerous signs of the final effects of the Eucharist. The twig emerging from the dead trunk that supports the roof of the shed at the left,[20] the shoots of laurel in the wall above the bystanders at the right, and the peacock on the same wall at the far right of the picture (Fig. 4) are all familiar symbols of resurrection and everlasting life. Botticelli's reworking of the Eucharistic symbolism entails more than just esthetic improvement and thematic amplification. For in doing away with the obviousness of the imagery of the earlier altarpiece he is able to reflect far more elastically the core of Eucharistic doctrine on which the conceptual structure of his painting rests.

A Eucharistic significance is implicit in any representation of the Epiphany.[21] Christ was revealed to the Magi in Bethlehem, the "city of bread." Of the gifts which the Magi offered there, one might signify Christ's priesthood and another that he was to be sacrificed.[22] As early as the fourth century the figures of the Magi were invoked as examples of Eucharistic devotion. Chrysostom formulates this idea in the following manner:

> This Body, even lying in a manger, Magi reverenced. Yea, men profane and barbarous, leaving their country and their home, both set out on a long journey, and when they came, with fear and great trembling worshipped him. Let us, then, at least imitate those barbarians, we who are citizens of heaven. For they indeed when they saw him but in a manger, and in a hut, and no such thing was in sight as thou beholdest now, drew nigh with great awe; but thou beholdest him

reenactment of Christ's sacrifice on Calvary (see below, note 114). On the significance of the gifts see Sturdevant, *Misterio*, pp. 80-84.

[20] On this motive, see Peebles, "The Dry Tree: Symbol of Death."

[21] On the association of the Epiphany and the Eucharist in art, see also Nilgen, "Epiphany"; and Philip, "The Prado Epiphany by Jerome Bosch," pp. 280, 286f.

[22] Sturdevant, pp. 80-84.

not in the manger but on the altar, not a woman holding
him in her arms, but the priest standing by, and the Spirit
with exceeding bounty hovering over the gifts set before us.
Thou dost not merely see this Body itself as they did, but
thou knowest also its power. . . .[23]

Here is set forth the idea of the mystical identity between the
Christian altar and the manger of Bethlehem, which was to remain current throughout the Middle Ages. Its persistence is
plain enough in the altarpiece attributed to Francesco d'Antonio
(Fig. 5).

On Epiphany Day is celebrated not only the visit of the Magi
to Bethlehem, but also the Baptism of Christ and the Marriage at
Cana, at which Christ revealed his divinity by turning water into
wine, the liquid of the Sacrament.[24] The Offertory prayer for
the Feast of the Epiphany is as follows:

We beseech thee, O Lord, graciously to behold the gifts of
thy Church: wherein is set forth no longer gold and frankincense and myrrh, but what by those gifts is declared and
sacrificed and received, even Jesus Christ thy Son our Lord.[25]

Here in the text of the Mass itself is brought out the parallel
between the offering of the Magi and the sacrifice of the Eucharist.[26]

[23] John Chrysostom, *Homilies on First Corinthians*, xxiv, 8 [Migne:
xxiv, 5], in *A Select Library*, XII, p. 143. See also Chrysostom, *De incomprehensibili Dei natura, etc.*, hom. vi: "De beato Philogeno," in Migne,
Patrologia Graeca, XLVIII, col. 753. (Darrell Davisson informed me of these
passages.)

[24] Kehrer, *Drei Könige*, I, pp. 47f. Apocryphally, Epiphany Day is also
the Feast of the Multiplication of the Loaves and Fishes (*ibid.*).

[25] Cited from Dix, *The Shape of the Liturgy*, p. 496.

[26] The Offertory chant for the Epiphany is Psalm 71:10-11 (most Biblical citations used here are from the *New Catholic Edition of the Holy
Bible*, New York, 1951):

The kings of Tharsis and of the islands shall offer presents, the kings
of the Arabians and of Saba shall bring gifts: and all the kings of the
earth shall adore him, all the nations serve him.

These verses were of course regarded as a prophecy of the visit of the
Magi to Bethlehem. Mainly on the strength of this prophecy the Magi
were believed, throughout the Middle Ages and beyond, to have been kings.

Ever since St. Augustine, the Magi have been looked upon by the Church as representatives of the people (*gentes*),[27] that is, the faithful.[28] In the later Middle Ages, in both sermons and treatises on the Mass, the example of the Magi is frequently cited as proof of why the faithful should offer during the divine service.[29] Since lay offerings of bread and wine had by then mostly fallen into disuse and offerings of money become the rule, such invocations of the example of the Magi must have seemed most cogent.[30] Let us review the manner in which the faithful in fact brought up their offerings during the service.

In the earliest times Christian worshippers might bring gifts in kind, that is, bread and wine, to the feast of thanksgiving and commemoration which the celebration of the Eucharist then entailed. Often they received Communion from the very gifts which they themselves had brought. Within a few centuries these voluntary offerings had become mandatory gifts to the poor and the Church. Still, they might be regarded as offerings to God or even oblations, and as such retained a part within the framework of the liturgy.[31]

Everywhere the offering of the people became increasingly stylized. In Rome, at the Offertory of the Mass, the people presented their gifts to the pope and his retinue.[32] Already the rule

[27] Kehrer, I, p. 34.

[28] Thus the Dominican theologian, Petrus de Palude (*Sermones de sanctis*, sermo xli): "Moraliter per hos tres reges significantur omnes electi fideles . . . "; and, referring to Isaiah (sermo xxxviii): "et dixit omnes [gentes] quia per istos tres reges significatur totum genus humanum de tribus filijs Noe propagatum."

[29] Petrus de Palude, *Sermones de sanctis*, xli: "Sed dicitur, quare obtulerunt [Magi] ei munera? Respondetur. . . . ut ostenderent eum esse Deum, qui, dixit, Exodo, xxij: 'Non apparebis in conspectu meo vacuus'; ideo quando apparemus coram Domino, ut audiendo Missam, debemus aliquid Deo offerre. . . ." Guglielmus Durandus, *Rationale divinorum officiorum*, IV, xxx, 34 (ed. Naples, 1859, p. 225): "Alius offert aurum, imitatus Magos, qui aurum Domino obtulerunt."

[30] Jungmann, *Mass*, II, pp. 12f.

[31] Jungmann, II, pp. 2f. Often the gifts were brought before the beginning of the service proper to a side room in the church. There the offerings necessary for the sacrifice might be selected for transferral to the altar at the Offertory of the Mass. Out of this use there developed ceremonies such as the Great Entrances of the Eastern and Gallican rites, in which the bread and wine, proleptically venerated as the Body and Blood of the Lord, were taken to the altar for consecration. (*Ibid.*, pp. 4-6.)

[32] Jungmann, II, pp. 6-8.

seems to have been that the laity should not directly handle the sacred elements: "The oblation designating the Body of Christ is offered up not with bare hands, but . . . in white napkins."[33] From the bread and wine of the people a suitable amount was placed on the altar for consecration and administration at Communion. While upon the altar (especially after their consecration) the offerings were often covered with a silk veil.[34]

At Rome this offertory rite was practiced as early as the seventh century and survived, at least in its general outlines, for about five hundred years.[35] In other churches of the West it became customary for the people to make their oblations in an offertory procession. This usually took place after the Credo— that is, just before or during the Offertory of the Mass—or else before Communion.[36] As a rule the bread to be offered up was carried in a little white cloth.[37] Since the practice of taking Communion was by now infrequent, the gifts were no longer intended for consecration. Hence the ministers who received them placed them not on the altar but on a table situated behind it.[38]

---

[33] De Berlendis, *De oblationibus*, p. 110, citing an ancient codex: "Oblata Corpus Christi designans non nudis manibus, sed fanonibus multo labore studiorum candidis offertur." The *Ordo Romanus II* has, "Offerunt cum fanonibus candidis" (*ibid.*).

[34] De Berlendis, pp. 129f.

[35] Jungmann, II, p. 7. A more highly stylized relic of the ceremony is observed even today in the rite of Milan. In the Milanese ceremony four *vecchioni*, two old men and two old women drawn from a special lay confraternity, are the representatives of the people. They wear a white linen cloth known as the "fanon," a long broad scarf one of the sides of which is sewn together leaving only enough space for the head to pass through. (King, *Liturgies*, pp. 386f.) Here, too, the rule is that the *vecchioni* may not touch the offerings with their bare hands. The bread and cruets of wine are held in the ends of the fanon and thus presented to the celebrant, who blesses the *vecchioni* with the formula, "May the Lord bless thee and this thy gift," makes the sign of the cross over the gift, and proffers his maniple to be kissed. (*Ibid.*, pp. 419-22, esp. 421f.) On Sundays and feasts of the Lord it was the custom during the Middle Ages for the men in the congregation to lay pieces of money on the altar, kissing the mensa after having made the sign of the cross. The bread and wine offered up by the *vecchioni* were once consecrated in the same service (*ibid.*, p. 420). In present usage the vessels containing the wafers to be consecrated are brought forward by the subdeacon, who covers them with the ends of a cloth worn around the neck known as the *continentia*. The cruets containing the wine and water, covered by *velo aliquo decente*, are carried by an acolyte. (*Ibid.*, p. 423.)

[36] Jungmann, II, pp. 9-26.   [37] Jungmann, II, p. 9.

[38] *Ibid.*

After making their offerings, the faithful might kiss the maniple or the stole of the celebrant, or else the corporal of the altar, an extended paten, or the foot of a crucifix. They might then receive a priestly blessing, such as "May thy sacrifice be acceptable to the almighty God."[39] Although the people rarely communicated, the connection between their offering and Communion remained firmly established in principle. Only those eligible to communicate were to make oblations.[40]

During the tenth and eleventh centuries, lay oblations in kind fell mostly into disuse. The faithful now brought oil, candles, utensils intended for the use of the church, and especially money.[41] Even deeds of land, covered with altar cloths, might be offered up as oblations.[42] At most High Masses the people's offering of bread and wine survived in symbolic form only—in the bringing forward of the elements for consecration by the subdeacon, their liturgical "representative."[43]

But lay offerings in kind did not die out altogether. In many places they continued to be prescribed for certain feast days.[44] In France, on the occasion of his coronation, the new king offered up not only gold but also the bread and wine from which he was subsequently communicated.[45] In addition to those that were

[39] Jungmann, II, p. 17.
[40] De Berlendis, *De oblationibus*, pp. 110, 363; Martène, *De antiquis Ecclesiae ritibus*, IV, p. 56; Thiers, *Traitez des cloches*, pp. 223f.
[41] Jungmann, II, p. 11.
[42] Jungmann, II, p. 11; De Berlendis, p. 174.
[43] The process of the dissociation of the people from the action of the Eucharist did not stop here. As the Church sought to reestablish the distinction between voluntary offerings and those made according to prescription, the offering of the people was set at the beginning of the service, the position it had once occupied in the Gallican rite. (Jungmann, II, pp. 14-16.) Only the sacred elements might be offered up during the Offertory, and these usually were brought forward by clerics only (*ibid.*, pp. 11f.). Thus the people became onlookers at, rather than participants in, the service proper. Instead of offering within the celebration of the Eucharist, the faithful in effect paid for it in advance. Soon, in the later Middle Ages, it became possible for one to "buy" Masses. Still, such donations continued to be regarded as sacrificial. Even the payments of stipends for priests were looked upon as oblations. (*Ibid.*, pp. 24f.) For in the eyes of the Church one might through "good works" such as these enhance one's chances of salvation. This rather Pelagian point of doctrine was of course soon to come under the attack of Martin Luther.
[44] Jungmann, II, pp. 21f.; De Berlendis, p. 363.
[45] Martène, II, p. 222. When kings made offerings in the presence of, or were coronated by, the pope, the rule was for them to kiss his foot (De Berlendis, p. 367).

prescribed, certain voluntary oblations in kind, some of which have survived into our own century, were made on special occasions.[46] Thus the laity might offer bread and wine at anniversary feasts, at Masses for the Dead,[47] or at votive Masses such as those in honor of a patron saint.

The Feast of the Epiphany was especially suited to lay offerings. Its Offertory chant is one of the very few in the Missal which express the idea of oblation: "The kings of Tharsis and of the islands shall offer presents. . . ."[48] During the eleventh century, apparently in France, there originated the liturgical Epiphany play. This play, often called the *Officium Stellae*, seems at first to have been a dramatized Offertory procession representing the journey of the Magi to Bethlehem and their offering to Christ.[49] The manger at Bethlehem was represented by an altar, upon which an image of the Madonna and Child was sometimes placed.[50]

With the passage of time the Epiphany play became increasingly secular in character. It was first removed from its position within the liturgy and finally taken outside of the church altogether.[51] But its association with the Eucharist must long have remained apparent. One hears of elaborate pageants with great secular processions at Milan in 1336 and at Fribourg (Switzerland) in 1417, in which the manger was still represented by an altar.[52] Florence, too, knew a splendid Epiphany pageant, the

[46] Jungmann, II, pp. 13, 23; De Berlendis, pp. 362f.

[47] See especially Thiers, *Traitez des cloches*, pp. 176-224.

[48] Jungmann, II, p. 30. The chant is from Psalm 71:10 (see above, note 26).

[49] On the *Officium Stellae*, see especially Young, *The Drama of the Medieval Church*, II, pp. 29-124; and Anz, *Die lateinischen Magierspiele*.

[50] For a discussion of the kinds of images which might be used for this purpose, see Forsyth, "Magi and Majesty." Kehrer (*Drei Könige*, I, p. 57) suggests that Christ's presence may at times have been conveyed by the consecrated host in a monstrance. This seems impossible in view of the fact that expositions of the host were unknown until the fourteenth century (see Browe, *Die Verehrung der Eucharistie im Mittelalter*, pp. 141-66).

[51] See Young, II, pp. 29-124; and Creizenach, *Geschichte des neueren Dramas*, I, *passim*. See also Nilgen, "Epiphany," p. 312.

[52] For a description of the Milanese pageant, see Galvano Fiamma, *De rebus gestis a . . . Vicecomitibus*, in *Rerum Italicorum scriptores*, XII, pp. 1017f. (also printed in A. d'Ancona, *Origini del teatro italiano*, 2nd ed., Turin, 1891, I, pp. 97f.). On the pageant at Fribourg, see Anz, p. 47; and Crombach, *Primitiae*, pp. 734f.

Festa de' Magi, which seems to have originated toward the end of the Trecento and been presented regularly until around 1470.[53] This pageant was connected with the church of San Marco, at which were preserved some "simulacra" of the manger. Its highpoint was a great procession from the Piazza della Signoria to the Piazza San Marco, where the Magi made their offerings to the Child. A public oblation was made at the church of San Marco on the same day.[54]

Some general conclusions may now be drawn about the offering of the people. Although it underwent several mutations, a number of its principal elements seem to have remained constant from the early Middle Ages until well after the era of the Counter Reformation. Whatever the nature of the gift that is offered up, it remains in doctrine a sacramental oblation, a "good work" that may in some way affect the workings of Grace. Where the offering is in kind, the layman does not ordinarily touch it with his bare hands but holds it in a white cloth. The act of offering on the part of the worshipper entails a symbolic act of love and homage toward Christ, usually a kiss, which is given either to the priest, the altar, a Eucharistic cloth or vessel, or a crucifix.[55] After the layman has performed his

[53] On the Festa de' Magi, see Hatfield, "Compagnia," pp. 108-119.

[54] Ibid., pp. 109, 136.

[55] The act of offering is also closely associated with the Kiss of Peace, in which Christ's love passes symbolically through the same agents—the priest, the altar, a Eucharistic vessel, a crucifix, or a special tablet representing Christ—to the worshipper. The Kiss of Peace is related to Matthew 5:24: "Leave thy gift before the altar and go first to be reconciled to thy brother, and then come and offer thy gift." On it, see Jungmann, Mass, II, pp. 321-32; and De Berlendis, De oblationibus, pp. 105-8. In medieval Epiphany plays the Magi sometimes meet and exchange the kiss of peace before proceeding to their interview with Herod (see Forsyth, "Magi and Majesty," p. 220, n. 39; and Young, Drama, II, passim). On the tablet representing Christ, often called the "pax brede," see Jungmann, II, pp. 328-30; De Berlendis, pp. 106-8; and Martène, De antiquis Ecclesiae ritibus, III, pp. 43, 222. A pax brede attributed to Fra Filippo Lippi, representing the Man of Sorrows, is in the Horne Museum in Florence (Catalogo della Mostra d'Arte Antica: Lorenzo il Magnifico e le arti, Florence, 1949, p. 26, no. 5). Such a tablet may have been used in a liturgical celebration, apparently invented by Savonarola, which took place at San Marco in Florence on Epiphany Day, 1498. In this celebration there were three separate adorations of the Child, in which each of the friars in the monastery took up the "Christ" and kissed respectively his foot, hand, and mouth. The ceremony is described in La vita del beato Ieronimo Savonarola scritta da un anonimo del secolo XVI e già attribuita a fra Pacifico Burlamacchi, ed. P. Ginori Conti, Florence, 1937, pp. 117f.

oblation he receives a blessing, often in the form of a priestly benediction. The offering of the people is closely tied to Communion, in which the worshipper, having consumed the Body of Christ—which the worshipper himself has in a sense offered up—is spiritually united with him. Thus the lay offering is a threefold action comprising oblation (a sacramental gift), adoration (a kiss addressed to Christ), and the receipt of unction (benediction or Communion). A Eucharistic action, it lends itself gracefully to figuration in terms of the Adoration of the Magi.

It should now be evident that the conceptual structure of Botticelli's altarpiece includes an allusion to the offering of the people, all of the principal motives of which are carefully referred to in the imagery of the painting. Although not unprecedented, the Eucharistic symbolism of Botticelli's altarpiece is quite unusual in Florentine paintings of the Adoration of the Magi.[56] Why should a Eucharistic meaning, always latent in the action of the Epiphany as the Church understood it, have here been made overt?

In the early days of the Church the celebration of the Eucharist was a participatory service founded upon the idea that the Church is a single body which worships in unison. The sacrifice was thought of as a corporate offering on behalf of all mankind.[57] But already in the early Middle Ages there had begun a gradual reduction of lay participation in the liturgy, which led to a lessening regard for the sacrifice as a corporate action and an increasingly subjective emphasis upon the physical presence of Christ under the appearances of the bread and wine.[58] In time, Christ became awesome in the host, until the layman hardly dared to consume him. Thus the worshipper's role was reduced to the passive one of seeing and hearing rather than doing.[59] One no longer sacrificed and partook of Christ's Body along

[56] Other paintings in which Eucharistic symbolism may be found are mentioned above, p. 36; see also note 13.

[57] Dix, *Shape*, p. 21. Cf. Romans 12:5: "so we, the many, are one body in Christ, but severally members one of another."

[58] Dix, p. 598; Jungmann, I, pp. 82-84, 118-21.

[59] Jungmann, II, pp. 359-67; Dix, p. 598.

with the universal Church, but offered up for one's personal
benefit.[60] No more regarded as the reenactment of the sacrifice
of Calvary on behalf of all men, the Mass acquired the par-
ticularistic function of relieving the worshipper from the burden
of his venial sins.[61] Still, the notion of the Eucharist as a corporate
action persisted. Even St. Thomas upholds the Pauline doctrine
that the "spiritual benefit received in the Sacrament is the unity
of the mystical Body."[62]

But in the fourteenth and fifteenth centuries one rarely hears
about Christ's Body as the essence of the Church or about the
Sacrament as its life and unity. Rather, Eucharistic debate was
now almost entirely centered upon the question of transubstanti-
ation, that is, the relation of the physical properties of the sacramental bread and wine to the real presence of Christ's Body and
Blood. As Jungmann has put it, "the *eucharistia* had become an
epiphania, an advent of God who appears among men and dis-
penses his graces."[63] There was thus encouraged an even more
individualistic and subjective bias in lay devotion, which became
increasingly obsessed with the Eucharist as it was now conceived.
The cult of the Eucharist, that is, the consecrated host, to which
great immediate powers were often attributed, spread rapidly.[64]
Great theophoric processions in honor of the Corpus Christi
became major events on the religious calendars of every city in
Western Europe. Popular forms of devotional service were introduced, in which the adoration of the Eucharist was stressed.[65]
In some places the layman was even permitted to kiss the con-
secrated host at Mass, but this practice was condemned by the
Church as superstition.[66]

[60] Dix, esp. p. 203.
[61] Dix, pp. 598f.
[62] Dix, p. 267.
[63] Jungmann, I, pp. 117f.
[64] On the cult of the Eucharist, see Browe, *Verehrung*; and Dumoutet,
Le Désir de voir l'hostie.
[65] At the same time the layman might no longer attend Mass in its en-
tirety. Rather, it was now common for the faithful to rush in just before
the moment of consecration, gaze in adoration upon the elevated host, and
then depart—often in order to assist at the moment of consecration in a
different Mass. (Browe, pp. 66-68; see also the Piovano Arlotto's account
of his celebration of Mass in one of the Florentine churches [*Motti e
facezie del piovano Arlotto*, pp. 81f.].)
[66] Browe, pp. 65f.

With this outburst of Eucharistic piety, Eucharistic symbolism quite naturally found its way into representations of the Epiphany. This seems to have occurred most often in paintings done in Germany and the Low Countries,[67] where innovations in Eucharistic devotion were especially common and the cult of the Magi especially strong. But the Northern paintings in which reference is made to the Eucharist have little in common pictorially with Botticelli's altarpiece. The pictorial source of Botticelli's Eucharistic imagery was local: the altarpiece attributed to Francesco d'Antonio (Fig. 5) or another painting like it. And Botticelli's inspiration to rework that source came, in all probability, from the Dominican friars of Santa Maria Novella and— if only indirectly—from the monastery of San Marco, the home of the Dominican Observants.

By a curious coincidence the Dominicans in Florence had the tutelage of the cults of both the Eucharist and the Epiphany in Botticelli's day. Their principal house, Santa Maria Novella, was responsible for the maintenance of dogma in the city. It staffed in large part the theological faculty of the university, then known as the Studio Fiorentino.[68] Of the doctrines which the *maestri di teologia* of Santa Maria Novella were promulgating during the second half of the Quattrocento, that of the Corpus Christi (or Corpus Domini) was probably the one which most occupied their thoughts. From its inception until the fourth decade of the Quattrocento, the Feast of Corpus Christi, in which every major religious and secular organization in the city took part, was held at Santa Maria Novella. Its high point was a huge procession in which the Blessed Sacrament was carried "enthroned" under a canopy through the streets of Florence.[69] But around 1432, four years before its consecration, the archbishop and canons of the

[67] On these paintings, see Nilgen, "Epiphany"; and Philip, "Prado Epiphany."

[68] On Santa Maria Novella, see Orlandi, *Necrologio*, esp. II, pp. 387-404; Richa, *Notizie*, III, pp. 1-109; Paatz, *Kirchen*, III, pp. 663-845; and Brown, *The Dominican Church of Santa Maria Novella at Florence*.

[69] During the procession in present usage the Blessed Sacrament is held aloft under a canopy by a priest wearing the humeral veil. On the celebration, see Fineschi, *Della festa e della processione del Corpus Domini in Firenze*. On Corpus Christi celebrations generally, see Browe, *Verehrung*, pp. 71-140. The Dominicans had the unique privilege of displaying the host from the Agnus Dei until Communion during the Mass (Browe, pp. 63f.).

Cathedral of Florence claimed the celebration for their own. A bitter litigation ensued, which became a major civic issue and even resulted in the closing of Santa Maria Novella for several months in 1459. The matter was referred to Rome and a compromise finally reached which enabled the monastery to retain some of its earlier prerogatives.[70]

Some of the *maestri* of Santa Maria Novella had been trained in northern Europe. One of them, Fra Lorenzo di Tommaso Gherardini, is believed to have taken his master's degree at the University of Cologne.[71] Cologne was the center of the cult of the Magi in western Europe. At Cologne Gherardini doubtless saw the procession in which three crowned priests representing the Magi, the city's patrons, carried the Sacrament.[72] He must also have become conversant there with the theological subtleties on which rested the association between the Epiphany and the Eucharist.[73] In 1470 Gherardini joined the College of Doctors at the Studio Fiorentino. He was prior of Santa Maria Novella from July 1474 to September 1476.

Another of the *maestri* of Santa Maria Novella was Fra Bartolommeo di Antonio Lapacci (de' Rimbertini).[74] Lapacci's assignments took him as far afield as Scandinavia and Greece, where he temporarily held two of the bishoprics then under Roman jurisdiction. He also visited Constantinople, where at the invitation of John VIII Paleologus he took part in public theological debates. At Constantinople he must have become familiar with the Eastern rite, with its Great Entrance, a procession in which the elements of the sacrifice, proleptically hailed as the "King of All Things," are taken to the altar for consecration while the congregation prostrate themselves in adoration.[75] Lapacci was also a prolific writer. Among his major works are tracts on the Incarnation, the Blood of the Crucified, and the distinction be-

[70] Fineschi, pp. 21-31.

[71] On Gherardini, see Orlandi, *Necrologio*, II, pp. 330-34.

[72] Réau, *Iconographie*, II, ii, p. 239.

[73] Gherardini also spent some years in France, as well as in England, where he was the confidant of Queen Margaret. In either of these countries he might have learned of the ceremonies in which their sovereigns imitated the Magi by making offerings of gold, frankincense, and myrrh at the altar on Epiphany Day (see below, Chapter III, p. 91).

[74] On Lapacci, see Orlandi, II, pp. 280-88.

[75] On the Great Entrance, see King, *Notes on the Catholic Liturgies*, pp. 422-25.

tween the Holy Spirit and the Son. Sermons of his are preserved on both the Eucharist and the Epiphany.

An even more prolific writer was Fra Giovanni di Carlo,[76] who chanced to be one of the friars who witnessed the drawing up of Guasparre dal Lama's first will, and also the prior who made the agreement with Angelica Malefici for the endowment of Guasparre's chapel.[77] One of his works is a commentary on the hymns to the Corpus Christi. He also composed the Office that was performed at Sant'Ambrogio in commemoration of the miracle which occurred there in 1230, when some wine accidentally left in a chalice after Mass turned to blood.[78] For this Office all of the friars of Santa Maria Novella went to Sant'Ambrogio, where they joined in the procession and other solemnities.[79]

The monastery of San Marco, which became the Florentine home of the Dominican Observants only in 1436,[80] seems to have had a longstanding association with the Epiphany.[81] The grandiose Epiphany pageant, the Festa de' Magi, was presented there from 1390 at the latest.[82] When the church was reconsecrated in 1443, the Feast of the Epiphany was chosen as the day for the ceremony.[83] San Marco seems always to have been the home of the Compagnia de' Magi, a religious lay confraternity devoted to the Three Kings. During the first six or seven decades of the Quattrocento the confraternity's chief occupation seems to have been the production of the Festa de' Magi.[84] After the pageant was discontinued around 1470, the brothers, doubtless stimulated by the efforts of the young Lorenzo de' Medici to provide the confraternity with an exceptional set of spiritual prerogatives—and

[76] On Fra Giovanni, see Orlandi, II, pp. 353-80.
[77] See above, Chapter I, p. 26.
[78] On the miracle, see Richa, *Notizie*, II, pp. 240f.
[79] Fra Giovanni also produced a book of *Lives* of the most eminent friars of Santa Maria Novella. It opens with a dedicatory letter to Cristoforo Landino, who was himself the author of a sermon on the "Body of Christ" that was read before the Compagnia de' Magi (on the sermon, see Hatfield, "Compagnia," pp. 130f.; on the Compagnia de' Magi, see below).
[80] On the early history of San Marco under the Dominican Observants, see Morçay, "La cronaca del convento fiorentino di San Marco." The chronicle (Laur., San Marco, 370) was written in 1506 by Roberto degli Ubaldini da Gagliano. The portion published by Morçay, eleven folios copied from an earlier chronicle by Giuliano Lapaccini covering the years until 1455, comprises less than one-tenth of the whole.
[81] Hatfield, "Compagnia," pp. 108f.
[82] *Ibid.*, p. 108.   [83] *Ibid.*, p. 136.   [84] *Ibid.*, pp. 108-22.

probably encouraged as well by the friars of San Marco—turned to activities of a more strictly devotional cast.[85] We possess no less than five sermons on the Eucharist that were written for delivery in the Compagnia de' Magi on Maundy Thursday, the Feast of the Last Supper.[86] One of them, by Pier Filippo Pandolfini and given on 11 April 1476, contains a passage reminiscent of Chrysostom's invocations of the Magi as exemplars of Eucharistic devotion:

> Let us humbly pray him that he plant in our hearts so much compunction, so much love, that we may be worthy to participate in his highest and supreme good, and that on the most holy day of Easter our souls may dine on his most precious food; for whoever tastes it properly shall not perish in all eternity. Gracious and benign Lord . . . make us worthy to receive this Sacrament for the salvation of our souls. May that bread and wine which this evening, father governor, as our master and in the figure of the Body and Blood of Christ, you have given to these brothers, fill up our souls and be the guide which leads us to that true and perpetual meal in the heavenly homeland where rules the One who is living. . . . May the splendor of that star which from Orient led the three Magi to adore and contemplate the divine majesty, light up our minds and lead us all to the true glory and supreme happiness. And in order that better and more deservedly we be hearkened to, let us offer this evening to Jesus Christ, imitating the holy Magi, the gold from the treasure of our minds . . . let us give him our souls . . . let us offer him the incense of our prayers . . . begging him devoutly that by virtue of his most holy Body and precious Blood, of which this evening we make special mention, he may have mercy on all this family.[87]

The governor of the confraternity was a layman. He had given to the brothers, probably at a fraternal meal in commemoration

[85] *Ibid.*, pp. 122-28.
[86] *Ibid.*, pp. 128-35.
[87] *Ibid.*, p. 156. Cf. the Collect of the Mass for the Epiphany: "O God, who on this day by the guidance of a star didst reveal thine only-begotten Son to the Gentiles: grant in thy mercy that we who know thee now by faith may be led even to contemplate the beauty of thy Majesty."

of the Last Supper,[88] both bread and wine, "the figure of the Body and Blood of Christ."[89] The offering which the brothers are to make is here a spiritual one which—even more than a material oblation—will prepare them for Communion and eventual salvation. Thus a more subjective dimension is added to the idea of oblation. But the principle is as before: the worshipper is called upon to imitate the examples of the Magi in terms of devotional practices with which he is familiar.

Had it been voiced in public, rather than in the privacy of the confraternity's oratory, the subjective slant in Pandolfini's address might have been found disquieting by the more institutionally-minded Dominicans. In matters of lay offerings it was not in their interests to stress the spiritual at the cost of the material.

In any case the material value of the gifts is not overlooked in Botticelli's altarpiece. Here was a combination of themes close to the heart of a Florentine Dominican: the Epiphany and the Eucharist. The painting may be seen as an exhortation to the worshipper both to offer to, and to adore the Body of Christ (as the old Magus is doing). But is the Body of Christ in Botticelli's picture just the agent of personal unction, the *bona gratia* of the Eucharistic conceptions of Botticelli's day? Or might it also be the mystical body of the Church, the corporate unity of which had once been the underlying idea of all liturgical action and indeed, only a few hundred years before Botticelli's time, one of the tenets in the doctrine of St. Thomas?

What kind of oblation is intended in Botticelli's picture? Is one to understand the scene as a corporate offering on the part of all of the faithful?

We beseech thee, O Lord, graciously to behold the gifts of thy Church: wherein is set forth no longer gold and frankincense and myrrh, but what by those gifts is declared and sacrificed and received, even Jesus Christ thy Son our Lord.[90]

[88] Hatfield, "Compagnia," p. 125.
[89] This phrase was a favorite of early writers on the Eucharist such as Tertullian and Ambrose (Jungmann, *Mass*, ii, pp. 187f.).
[90] Offertory prayer of the Mass for the Epiphany (Dix, *Shape*, p. 496).

Or is the scene to be understood as a private offering, by and on behalf of Guasparre dal Lama,[91] who appears to be portrayed as the old man looking out from the group of bystanders at the right of the picture (Figs. 4, 53)?[92] Perhaps no answer is needed. Corporate and private may here be the same thing.

The Lord whom ye seek shall suddenly come to his temple.
—Malachi 3:1

Any representation of the Epiphany is implicitly an allegory of the Church. Liturgically the Epiphany is the day on which the Church is married to Christ. At its Lauds and Hours the antiphon to the Benedictus goes:

Today the Church is joined to her celestial spouse, because in Jordan Christ doth wash her sins; the Magi hasten with gifts to the royal marriage feast, and the guests exult in the water turned to wine.[93]

The idea that the Magi had a role in Christ's union to his Church is one that goes back to its earliest fathers. The Magi have always been looked upon as forerunners of the community of the faithful. For Augustine, Christ is the *lapis angularis*,[94] the cornerstone that joins together both Jews and pagans in a universal religion. Christ was first seen by the shepherds—Jews. And the Magi were the *primitiae gentium*, the first of the Gentiles to whom he was revealed. Augustine understands them figuratively, in the broadest possible sense, as the representatives not only of the orient but of the whole world. Their church is the *universa Ecclesia gentium*. In celebrating the Epiphany, Christians—converted

[91] By the terms of his first testament votive Masses were to have been said at Guasparre's altar on Epiphany Day. In both his second and third testaments an anniversary feast (*annuale*) with Mass for the Dead was envisioned. Yearly Masses for the Dead for Guasparre's soul were also provided for in the agreement between Angelica Malefici and the prior of Santa Maria Novella. At any of these functions lay offerings in kind might have been performed.

[92] On Guasparre's identity, see below, Chapter III.

[93] *Catholic Encyclopedia*, 1909, v, p. 506. See also Kehrer, *Drei Könige*, I, pp. 46-49.

[94] Cf. Psalm 117:22; Isaiah 28:16; Matthew 21:42-44; Luke 20:17-18.

Gentiles—thus commemorate the origin of their own Church.⁹⁵
In time Augustine's ideas were developed by other theologians.
The Magi were firmly identified with the *omnes gentes* of the
seventy-first psalm, the nations of the world who would become
the servants of Christ. They were even traced back to the three
sons of Noah.⁹⁶ Thus by the later Middle Ages the Magi, the
primitiae gentium, were firmly established as personifications of
the Christian faith as a whole. In the altarpiece for Guasparre dal
Lama, Botticelli seems clearly to have expatiated upon this idea
of Christ's union with the faithful, that is, his Church. He has
done so especially in his handling of the background, in which
he develops the motive of the ruin.

From the earliest times Christian theologians have interpreted
Christ's Incarnation as the fulfilment of Old Testament prophecies
of the restoration of the Old Temple. One of these is the prophecy of Amos (9:11):

> In that day will I raise up the tabernacle of David that is
> fallen; and I will close up the breaches of the walls thereof,
> and repair what was fallen; and I will rebuild it as in the
> days of old that they may possess the remnant of Edom and
> all nations, because my name is invoked upon them.

The Tabernacle of David of course was the predecessor of the
Temple of Solomon, which itself eventually fell into ruin. Exegesis provided additional sources on which images of ruinous
buildings might be based. Bethlehem was the city of David, the
ancestor of Christ. Thus the stable in which Christ was born was
supposed to have been David's hut. And near it, according to
legend, was his palace.⁹⁷

⁹⁵ On Augustine's interpretation of the Epiphany, see Kehrer, I, p. 34.
⁹⁶ Petrus de Palude, *Sermones de sanctis*, xxxviii: "per istos tres reges
significatur totum genus humanum de tribus filijs Noe propagatum." See
also Crombach, *Primitiae*, p. 75; and Hatfield, "Compagnia," p. 120, n. 51.
⁹⁷ Except for the shed, these buildings seem to be clearly indicated in
Northern paintings only. The crumbling building in Conrad Witz's
Adoration of the Magi at Geneva (Fig. 9) may stand for either the Syna-
gogue or the Palace of David (for a group of related motives, see Kehrer,

These buildings might all be imagined to have been in decay at the moment of Christ's birth, through which they were to be cleansed. A medieval legend tells of a Roman building, the Templum Pacis, which was still intact. When, during the reign of Augustus, Rome had been at peace for twelve years, an oracle was asked how much longer the peace would last. The oracle's reply, that there would be peace until a virgin should bear a child, quite naturally was taken to mean forever; and so, in celebration, a temple was built and the words, "Eternal Temple of Peace," inscribed over its doors. On the night of Christ's birth, however, the Templum Pacis collapsed into ruins.[98]

In Florence the legend of the Templum Pacis seems to have been quite popular.[99] The columns in Alberti's additions to the facade of Santa Maria Novella appear to be based on a column from the Basilica of Maxentius, which building Alberti's patron, Giovanni Rucellai, thought to be the Templum Pacis.[100] The Templum Pacis is known to have been represented by a float in

---

ii, pp. 250-69). David's Palace is depicted in the central panel of the Portinari Triptych by Hugo van der Goes (Fig. 66; see Panofsky, *Early Netherlandish Painting*, p. 334). On the iconography of such buildings in representations of the Nativity and the Epiphany, see Panofsky, p. 135; Cornell, *The Iconography of the Nativity of Christ*, pp. 42f.; and Philip, "Prado Epiphany," pp. 269 and 281, n. 62.

[98] On the site of the Templum Pacis there later rose the church of Santa Maria Nuova. See Jacobus de Varagine, *Legenda Aurea*, vi: "De Nativitate Domini . . ." (ed. T. Graesse, p. 42), citing Innocent III, *Sermones de sanctis*, ii: "In Nativitate Domini" (Migne, *Patrologia Latina*, ccxvii, cols. 457f.). See also Crombach, p. 235.

[99] On the iconography of the Templum Pacis, see Cornell, pp. 42f.; Warburg, *Gesammelte Schriften*, I, pp. 156f., 362f.; and Chastel, *Art et humanisme*, p. 239. Before 1500 there seems to have been little agreement about the appearance of the Templum Pacis. One tradition, possibly originating with Flavio Biondo, identified it with the Basilica of Maxentius (see Warburg, I, pp. 156, n. 1, and 362f.). In the notebook of Buonaccorso Ghiberti (BNC, Banco Rari, 228, fol. 35v) it is shown as a tall, domed cylindrical structure to which a portico and a tall parallelopiped with squat protruding "apse" are attached. A representation of the Templum Pacis as a kind of monopteros is found in *A Florentine Picture-Chronicle . . . by Maso Finiguerra*, ed. S. Colvin, pl. xxxvii (I owe this information to Philip Foster). On an elaboration, apparently devised by Fontius, on the imagery of Christ's triumph over the heathen world in a painting of Ghirlandaio's, see Saxl, "The Classical Inscription in Renaissance Art and Politics," pp. 28f.

[100] Warburg, I, pp. 362f. The column is now in Santa Maria Maggiore in Rome.

the procession of the *edifizi* for the Feste di San Giovanni, Florence's principal holiday, as early as 1454.[101]

Strictly speaking, these ruins are proper to the Nativity only. However, the most frequently cited prophecy of the Epiphany, that of Balaam, also conveys the idea of ruin:

> A star shall rise out of Jacob, and a sceptre (virgin) shall spring up from Israel and shall strike the chiefs of Moab, and shall waste all the children of Seth.[102]

Both theologically and liturgically, moreover, the Epiphany is closely related to the Nativity,[103] of which it may be seen as the necessary consequence. One may even think of it as the "thirteenth day" of Christmas (with which feast it was once identical). For the Old Testament foretells that the Gentiles and the Semites shall converge at the coming of the Messiah.[104] The Nativity thus signifies Christ's Incarnation and his appearance to the Jews, and the Epiphany his revelation to the Gentiles, without which his advent could not have been complete. The two events, then, mark the opening and completion of a single action. And in fact ruins first appear in representations of both the Nativity and the Epiphany at roughly the same time.

These ruins, most of which belong to the province of legend, might never have found their way into religious imagery were it not for some texts from the Gospels to which they are well suited. One of these is in Luke (2:34):

> Behold, this child is destined for the fall (*ruinam*) and for the rise (*resurrectionem*) of many in Israel, and for a sign that shall be contradicted.

101 Hatfield, "Compagnia," p. 114, n. 40. The float was the eleventh on the program and was used for a Nativity play. Twelfth on the program was an octangular temple with the seven virtues, Herod, and, at the side, Mary and Jesus. Thirteenth were the Magi with a cavalcade of two hundred followers.

102 Numbers 24:7. "Virgin" (*virgo* instead of *verga*) was the reading usually accepted during the Middle Ages.

103 In many respects the Offices for the Epiphany recall those for Christmas. On the theological association of the Nativity and the Epiphany, see Crombach, *Primitiae, passim;* Kehrer, *Drei Könige,* I, *passim;* and Réau, *Iconographie,* II, ii, pp. 214, 231.

104 Crombach, pp. 73-82. Cf. Augustine's interpretation of the Epiphany.

This prophecy, spoken by Simeon upon Christ's presentation in the temple, is the first verse of the Gospel that is read at Mass on Sunday within the Octave of the Nativity, one of the more important feasts that fall between Christmas and the Epiphany. The text lends itself nicely to disquisitions on what lies in store for those who do not follow Christ as opposed to that which awaits those who do. In sermons for Sunday within the Octave of the Nativity by Dominican writers of the later Middle Ages the stress is upon the *ruinam* of unbelievers and the *resurrectionem* of the faithful: God humiliated the Jews, who were blind, and raised up the Gentiles, who had come into Israel—that is, accepted Christ—in great numbers.[105] Christ is the nemesis of the proud and the destroyer of whatever evil has been erected against God.[106] For Isaiah had prophesied that he should break the images of Egypt—wipe out all vices and sin.[107] The prophecy of Simeon lent itself quite naturally to imagistic explications. By vicariously making seven circuits of the walls of Jericho, the worshipper is told, he may bring down the evil that resides within him.[108] In their weakness men are like leaning walls which may fall into ruin.[109] But if they will support themselves upon God they shall

[105] Petrus de Palude, *Sermones de tempore*, xxviii ("Dominica infra octavas Nativitatis Christi"): "Jpse enim superbos Iudeos humiliavit, et Gentiles humiles exaltavit. Unde Romanis, xj: 'Cecitas contigit ex parte in Israel donec plenitudo gentium intraret.'" (Romans 9:30-33; 11:1-29.) Cf. also Isaiah 8:14-15: "And he shall be a sanctification to you: but for a stone of stumbling, and for a rock of offense to the two houses of Israel, for a snare and a ruin to the inhabitants of Jerusalem. And very many of them shall stumble and fall, and shall be broken in pieces, and shall be snared and taken."

[106] Petrus de Palude, *Sermones de tempore*, xxviii: "Nam ipse est humilium erector et superborum prostrator." Sermo xxx: "quicquid male contra Deum erectum fuerat dissipet et disperdet."

[107] *Ibid.*, xxx: "ingredietur Egyptum, id est in hunc mundum vicijs tenebrosum, et movebuntur simulachra Egypti, id est ruent vicia et peccata quibus humana natura erat subiecta." Cf. Osee 10:2 (of Israel): "Their heart is divided, now they shall perish: he shall break down their idols, he shall destroy their altars."

[108] Petrus de Palude, *Sermones de tempore*, xxx.

[109] Jacobus de Varagine, *Sermones de tempore*, iii ("In Dominicam infra octavas Nativitatis Domini"): "Appodiant se rei exposite casui, ideo assimilantur parieti inclinato." Cf. Isaiah 30:12-13: "Because you have rejected this word, and have trusted in oppression and tumult, and have leaned upon it; therefore shall this iniquity be to you as a breach that falleth, and is found wanting in a high wall, for the destruction thereof shall come on a sudden, when it is not looked for."

be saved, for God is like a rock or a mountain.[110] The sign which shall be contradicted is of course that of Christ himself. It appears over a mountain, which represents the world.[111]

Later in his life, citing one of the prophecies of David,[112] Christ was to allude to himself as the destroyer of disbelief:

> The stone which the builders rejected has become the corner stone; by the Lord this has been done, and is it wonderful in our eyes? Therefore I say to you that the kingdom of God will be taken away from you and will be given to a people yielding its fruits. And he who falls on this stone will be broken to pieces; but upon whomever it falls, it will grind him to powder.[113]

Christ is here the cornerstone of which Augustine was to make so much in his exegesis of the Epiphany, the agent once again of both ruin and raising up.[114]

[110] Jacobus de Varagine, *Sermones de tempore*, iii: "Qui autem appodiat se Deo cadere non potest, quia appodiat se petre firmissime contra fluxibilitatem. . . . Appodiat se monti contra casus facilitatem." Isaiah also likens the Messiah to a rock (see above, note 105).

[111] Jacobus de Varagine, *Sermones de tempore*, iii: "Istud autem signum est Christus de quo dicitur Esaye, xiij: 'Super montem caliginosum levate signum.' Mons caliginosus est mundus qui errore excecatus prospera mundi tanquam vera bona appetebat et adversa tanquam vera mala refugiebat. Sed super istum montem caliginosum levatum est signum in quo tria sunt scripta et depicta, scilicet humilitas, paupertas et carnis asperitas. De quo dicitur Luce, ij [describing the Nativity]: 'Et hoc vobis signum invenietis infantem esse. . . .'"

[112] Psalm 117:22.

[113] Matthew 21:42-44; see also Luke 20:17-18. Cf. Isaiah 28:16: "Therefore thus saith the Lord God: Behold I will lay a stone in the foundations of Sion, a tried stone, a corner stone, a precious stone, founded in the foundation. He that believeth, let him not hasten."

[114] There was yet a third passage from the Gospels to which images of ruins might be related, in which Christ, having driven the tradesmen from the temple, prophesies his resurrection to the Pharisees (John 2:19-22; cf. Matthew 26:61):

> In answer Jesus said to them, "Destroy this temple and in three days I will raise it up." The Jews therefore said, "Forty-six years has this temple been in building, and wilt thou raise it up in three days?" But he was speaking of the temple of his body. When, accordingly, he had risen from the dead his disciples remembered that he had said this, and they believed the Scripture and the word that Jesus had spoken.

Christ's death and resurrection are not wholly unrelated to the Epiphany. For the myrrh which the Magi brought him was, to the Middle Ages, a

In Botticelli's altarpiece there is abundant reference to the fall and rise, *ruinam* and *resurrectionem*, of which Christ is the cause. The signs of ruin are perhaps the most prominent features in the setting of the painting. But as we have already had occasion to observe,[115] there are at least three manifest symbols of resurrection: the twig in the trunk which supports the shed, the shoots of laurel in the wall toward the right,[116] and the peacock on the same wall at the extreme right (Fig. 4)—at the very point to which is attached the beam which supports the canopylike roof. The wall, in the form of a corner, may itself be intended as a sign of resurrection through Christ's foundation of his Church. Within the shed, in the very center of the picture, rises the rock. In this context it may be the symbol of God (or Christ)—for

---

sign of his sacrificial death (see above, note 15). In the Quattrocento, moreover, it seems to have been believed widely that the Star of Bethlehem had revealed his Crucifixion to the Magi. In a sermon read before the Compagnia de' Magi, perhaps a few years after 1482, Giorgio Antonio Vespucci puts it thus: "And to our patrons, the most holy Magi, it was signified by that wonderful star, in which, one reads, and as pious opinion has it, they are believed already to have seen his most burdensome cross prefigured so many times" (Hatfield, "Compagnia," pp. 132f.). Christ's prophecy of his own resurrection might thus be taken as a statement about the significance of his Epiphany. For the temple which he would raise up was, as the evangelist points out, that of his own body. And Christ's Body is, mystically, the Church, which was founded at his Epiphany. If present, the symbolism may here operate in a double sense. For as nearly every medieval commentator on the Mass tells us, Christ's sacrifice of his own body on Calvary is the basic prototype of the celebration of the Eucharist: the Mass, with its offering, consecration, and consumption of the sacrifice, is nothing less than a symbolic reenactment of Christ's passion, resurrection, and redemption of mankind (Jungmann, *Mass*, I, pp. 86-88, 108-17). Through Christ's "Body"—the Eucharist as well as the Church—man may hope, if only he will offer of himself, for salvation.

[115] Above, p. 41. On the ruins in Botticelli's painting, see also Hartt, *History*, p. 282.

[116] It seems probable that the plants in question are laurel (*laurus nobilis*), since laurel in fact bears during the Christmas season the small berries that one sees in the altarpiece. The use of laurel as a Christian symbol of eternity or resurrection is probably due to St. Paul, who contrasts the laurel wreaths with which victorious pagans were crowned to the imperishable wreath which the faithful Christian would receive (I Corinthians 9:24-27). There is a possibility, however, that the plants in the altarpiece represent myrtle. In this case the allusion would be to the Gentiles' acceptance of Christ, in accordance with Zacharias 1:8: "I saw by night, and beheld a man riding upon a red horse, and he stood among the myrtle trees that were in the bottom; and behind him there were red horses, speckled, and white."

Joseph is supporting himself upon it—or of the world, that is, the universal Church.[117] And over the whole scene there shines the Star of Bethlehem, the sign of Christ.[118] As Isaiah had prophesied, "Behold I will lift up my hand to the Gentiles and will set up my sign to the people."[119] Christ would do so again at his Ascension, when, as his sign itself, he imparted his blessing to mankind.[120]

Botticelli's painting is not the earliest Florentine altarpiece of the Epiphany in which ruins are shown, but it is the first in which they are given real prominence. There is a ruined building, perhaps intended as David's Palace, in Gentile da Fabriano's altarpiece for Palla Strozzi of 1423 (Fig. 10). Another is found in the painting attributed to Francesco d'Antonio (Fig. 5). But before the time of the altarpiece for Guasparre dal Lama, the motive of the ruin seems to have been confined chiefly to pictures intended for private devotion.[121] It first becomes prominent in the Cook tondo by Fra Filippo Lippi, of perhaps around 1455,[122] which may have been commissioned by the Medici (Fig. 11).[123] Whether the ruins in the tondo stand for any particular buildings, seems im-

[117] On the rock as a symbol of Christ see above, note 17. The use of a rock, in many cultures a symbol of the Earth, to symbolize the Church is of course based on Christ's charge to St. Peter (Matthew 16:18-20): "et super hanc petram aedificabo Ecclesiam meam."

[118] In the chapel of the Medici Palace the Star has the form of the monogram of St. Bernardino of Siena, that is, the "IHS" of Christ.

[119] Isaiah 49:22.

[120] Petrus de Palude, *Sermones de tempore*, xxx: "hoc factum est in ascensione cum elevatus in celum benedixit eis."

[121] Prominent ruins do appear in a small panel, probably from a predella, of the *Adoration* by Giovanni dal Ponte in the gallery of the Courtauld Institute at London (which was brought to my attention by Darrell Davisson).

[122] At one time Berenson, followed by a number of other critics, believed that the Cook tondo was begun by Fra Angelico. However, he later retracted this opinion (Berenson, "Postscript, 1949: The Cook Tondo Revisited").

[123] It may be identical with a painting thought to be by Angelico in an inventory taken of the Medici Palace in 1492: "Uno tondo grande cholle chornice atorno messe d'oro, dipintovi la nostra Donna e el nostro Signore e e' Magi che vanno a offerire, di mano di fra Giovanni, f. 100" (Müntz, *Les Collections des Médicis au quinzième siècle*, p. 60).

possible to determine. In any event it seems clear that they represent religion which is corrupt and which Christ is to purify.[124]

Botticelli twice used the motive of the ruin in paintings of the Adoration which he appears to have done for private locations.[125] Both pictures are at London. One of them, probably done some years before the altarpiece for Guasparre dal Lama, is oblong in format (Fig. 12). In it the shed is set into a church of which the portico is intact. The ruined parts of the building probably stand for the Old Temple and the portico for the New. The ruins of two other buildings are also apparent.

The other picture is a tondo which Botticelli may have painted for Antonio Pucci (Figs. 14, 15).[126] The tondo may have been done a few years before the altarpiece. Here the ruins have become the proud remains of an ancient church. In the foremost of its arches the keystone has slipped out of joint. This church might be the Templum Pacis, since the building, although destroyed, seems recently built. But it might as easily be the Tabernacle of David.[127] In any case the roof of the shed, seen frontally

[124] Professor Joseph Polzer has suggested to me that the pheasant in the Cook tondo probably represents sloth, pointing out that the pheasant looks down, whereas the peacock, symbolizing eternity and redemption, has its head raised. If this is so, the Cook tondo may be seen as a moral allegory based on a set of oppositions of the Old Law to the New: pheasant against peacock, ass against ox (on their significance, see Réau, Iconographie, II, ii, pp. 228f.; and Panofsky, Early Netherlandish Painting, p. 278, n. 1), Old Temple against New, and "naked" persons (who have not yet accepted Christ and whose attitudes do not seem devout) against the followers of the Magi. The naked figures have been studied by Eisler ("The Athlete of Virtue: The Iconography of Asceticism," pp. 87f.). I do not accept his conclusions about them, which rest on a set of incorrect assumptions about the authorship, date, and origins of the picture. To me the naked figures do not look like athletes. In Quattrocento paintings such figures usually stand for man in a primitive condition, that is, persons who lived before the Mosaic Law (here, more properly, they would be persons living without Grace), or else for neophytes awaiting baptism.

[125] On these paintings, see Davies, The Earlier Italian Schools, pp. 97f., 101f.

[126] Davies, p. 102; Salvini, Botticelli, I, pp. 44f. Antonio Pucci was the Medici supporter for the marriage of whose son Botticelli and his assistants did the Wedding Feast of Nastagio degli Onesti (Fig. 13), which was sold by Christie's at London on 23 June 1967.

[127] Or conceivably it alludes to the Temple of Solomon. As has been noted, Botticelli's composition may owe something to Ghiberti's Visit of the Queen of Sheba to Solomon on the east doors of the Baptistry (see

within the ruins, has for all its humility the dignity to represent the Church. Of the two walls in the foreground, the one at the left is perceptibly worn; its corner is obscured by one of the figures. The other wall is smooth and new; its corner stands out sharply against the ground behind. These walls must refer to the "stone which the builders rejected," that is, Christ, who has here become the cornerstone, the *lapis angularis* of Augustine's teaching about the Epiphany.[128] They are perhaps to be understood in terms of the ancient religions: unreconciled and corrupt at the left, and properly conjoined at the right through the Child who has been revealed.

In the altarpiece for Guasparre dal Lama the great building has been placed in the background at the left, where it stands apart from the place of Christ's birth. The center of the picture is taken up by a rock which is evidently derived from that in the Cook tondo (Fig. 11). Since Botticelli's picture was destined for the facade wall of Santa Maria Novella, it seems possible that an allusion to the Templum Pacis is intended in the building at the left.[129] If so, the jagged corner of wall to which the shed is attached and which here serves as the "altar" may belong to the Tabernacle of David. But perhaps it is simply the "stone which the builders rejected," which here has become the foundation of the Church. Or could it be that the ruins, like those in all the paintings here under discussion, reflect a conflation of a number of these thoughts? For even here Botticelli, like Fra Filippo before him, gives no definite clue to the identity of the buildings. To have done so would have meant locating them within the esthetic context of legend and the apocrypha, as Northern painters sometimes did. Botticelli's buildings, it should be clear, belong to the province of doctrine.

Salvini, I, p. 44). In the Middle Ages a building near the shed of Christ's birth might be imagined to have been Solomon's Palace (quite logically, since Solomon was the son of David; see Philip, "Prado Epiphany," p. 281, n. 62). The Queen of Sheba's visit to Solomon was generally regarded as a prototype of the Epiphany (Crombach, *Primitiae*, p. 154).

[128] The motive of the corner also occurs in northern paintings, e.g., in a Netherlandish altarpiece of about 1480 in the Alte Pinakothek at Munich (ill.: Kehrer, *Drei Könige*, II, p. 283).

[129] However, it should be kept in mind that the figures at its base are shepherds, the representatives of the Jews.

In both the tondo and the altarpiece, the great temple—although by no means archeologically accurate in representation—seems remarkably classical in character. Although physically corrupt, its formal dignity is intact. In the terms of Edwin Panofsky these are the first ancient ruins which retain the full grandeur of classical "content." In earlier depictions there is always some ambiguity in the way they are shown. But here one may look upon them as reminders of the glories of ancient civilization—the culture of the Gentiles.

For St. Augustine, the Magi were the *primitiae gentium*, the "first of the Gentiles." As such they had a major role in the origins of Christian belief. But in the Bible, words based on the root *gens* have a number of pejorative connotations, some of which lingered throughout the Middle Ages. Even the Magi were often regarded with mixed feelings.[130] In the Florentine Quattrocento, however, the Gentiles came to be seen with some objectivity, in "perspective." "Gentiles" and its derivatives might now be used as purely descriptive terms, without implicit value judgments.[131] More important, the word was firmly reassociated with another of common root. That word is "gentility," which has always served to describe the social graces. The Gentiles, that is, the ancients, were now looked upon as models of cultured behavior. And so they have been ever since.

But if the Gentiles might serve as models in secular affairs, they were still unbelievers. How might Botticelli, in religious pictures, have conferred upon temples like theirs the dignity of an "Idea" of religion? The answer would lie in the revival of syncretic theology then being carried out by Marsilio Ficino and his followers. The errors of the Gentiles were understandable, Ficino argued, since they had not lived under Grace. But they did possess "natural" philosophy and religion, which hold out the same

---

130 Thus for Chrysostom they were "men profane and barbarous" (above, p. 41). Jacobus de Varagine says of them, "Voluit autem Deus primitiae gentium vocare potius ab oriente quam ab alia regione. Ex eo quod regio orientalis erat odiosa ac immunda et maledicta" (*Sermones de sanctis*, lvi: "De Epiphania Domini sermo i").

131 Thus Vespasiano da Bisticci, speaking of Cosimo de' Medici: "Ebbe buonissima perizia nelle lettere latine, così delle sacre come de' gentili" (*Vite di uomini illustri del secolo XV*, ed. P. d'Ancona and E. Aeschlimann, p. 405). See also N. Tommaseo and B. Bellini, *Dizionario della lingua italiana*, ii, 2, pp. 1036f.

truths—if under different guises—to all peoples. Like the He-
brews, they too might have a premonition of Christ.[132]

Botticelli's altarpiece may thus be seen as an allegory of the
Church, rising amidst the ruins of the ancient religions. To it
have flocked the Magi, representing the nations of the pagan
world, while the shepherds, representing the Jews, are seen in
the background at the left. It should now be clear that Christ's
Body, which he himself once refers to as a temple,[133] is in this
context the body of the Church. Botticelli's picture, it seems,
alludes to the Eucharist in both of its principal senses: as that food
which leads each believer to the eternal life and as that celebration which binds together the whole of Christianity. The doctrine of the Eucharist, that is, Christ's Body, is at the heart of
the conceptual structure of Botticelli's painting. It is the common term which has enabled him to conjoin the idea of the sacrificial offering (and its consequences)[134] with that of the Church
as a whole.

But that is not all. As an historical event the Epiphany was
thought to have occurred in Bethlehem either thirteen days or
two years and thirteen days from the date of Christ's birth. Yet
it is here attended—and in part perhaps enacted as well[135]—by a
number of persons who lived in Florence in the fifteenth century.
As it permits a conflation of separate actions, the doctrine of the
Eucharist permits a suspension of the unities of time and place.
For according to the Bible, the Eucharist fulfills all of the past

[132] Ficino's apology for the religious beliefs of the ancients has important antecedents in St. Thomas's theory of the implicit faith of the worthy
pagans and in the insistence upon the monotheism of the great ancient
poets by militant classicists of the early Quattrocento such as Francesco
da Fiano (see Baron, *The Crisis of the Early Italian Renaissance*, I, pp.
272-82). On Ficino's attitude toward ancient religions, see Kristeller, *The
Philosophy of Marsilio Ficino*, pp. 23-29, 314-23; and Chastel, *Marsil Ficin
et l'art*, pp. 157-60. On Ficino's view of the Magi, see Chastel, *Art et
humanisme*, pp. 246f.

[133] See above, note 114.

[134] On the possible allusions to Christ's own sacrifice, see above, p. 40
and note 114.

[135] The elder Magi in Botticelli's picture appear to be members of the
Medici family (see below, Chapter III).

and looks forward to beyond the end of time.[136] Thus the faithful may always be present at Christ's epiphany.[137] "Where is he that has been born the king of the Jews?"[138] the devout of Botticelli's day might have asked in emulation of the Magi. The answer was one which they no doubt knew. He is always present, sacramentally, in the Eucharist.[139]

Botticelli's altarpiece may thus be said to be synoptic, in that it represents different actions, places, and perhaps also people as one; and synchronous, in that it represents different moments as one. It seems susceptible to numerous interpretations. But these interpretations, however divergent initially, ultimately resolve in a single, fundamental chord. For the painting is tuned to the "well-tuned lyre" of the doctrine of the Body of Christ.[140] If any of its strings is plucked, the others will reverberate in sympathy. Botticelli's success in "tuning" his picture to Eucharistic doctrine has to do not with the abundance of obscure symbols sometimes used by the Northern painters, but with the unobtrusive density of its symbolic structure. The symbolic images in the picture are relatively few; and their approximate meanings must have been perfectly intelligible to the average worshipper (even if he may not have been equipped to appreciate their full significance). But a number of these images appear to convey more than a single thought—or, to return to the metaphor of the lyre, their overtones vary as the different "strings" of the picture are plucked. It is, then, the manner in which *familiar* images are interrelated—the fineness of its "tuning"—which sets Botticelli's painting apart. For an altarpiece in the form of a self-contained narrative picture it is perhaps unprecedented in the elasticity and range of its symbolic content.

---

[136] Dix, *Shape*, p. 4.

[137] On the Eucharist as an epiphany, see Jungmann, *Mass*, I, pp. 117f.; II, p. 141.

[138] Matthew 2:2.

[139] Petrus de Palude, *Sermones de sanctis*, xxxix: "Sexto potest queri ubi est sacramentaliter. Ad hoc respondetur sub specie panis et vini secundum quem modum nobiscum est in hac vita et semper erit."

[140] (I owe this metaphor to E. H. Gombrich.)

III

The Portraits

A GREAT SOURCE of fascination in Botticelli's altarpiece has been the portraits it is presumed to contain. These are first mentioned by the Anonimo Magliabechiano, who, however, does not name any of the persons represented.[1] In his first edition of the *Lives* (1550), Giorgio Vasari identifies two of them. "And the figure of [the old] king," he says, "is the very portrait of Cosimo de' Medici il Vecchio, the most lifelike and natural of those that are to be found in our day" (Fig. 27).[2] Vasari is demonstrably mistaken in saying that Botticelli here painted the "very portrait" of Cosimo, since the banker-statesman died in 1464.[3] However, most subsequent critics have agreed that the old Magus in fact represents him.

Vasari then turns to the Magus in the center (Fig. 3): "The second [king], who is Giuliano de' Medici, father of Pope Clement VII, is seen with all intentness of mind most devoutly doing reverence to that child and making over his gift to him."[4] But the central Magus can hardly represent Giuliano, who was murdered in 1478 when only twenty-four.[5]

In his second edition of the *Lives* (1568), Vasari gives the identity of the last king: "The third, who is also kneeling and who appears in adoring [the Child] to render him thanksgiving and confess him the true Messiah, is Giovanni, the son of Cosi-

---

[1] *Il Codice magliabechiano*, pp. 104f.: "una tavoletta . . . de' Magi che vi sono più persone ritratte al naturale."

[2] *Vite*, 1550, p. 493 (Vasari-Milanesi, III, p. 315).

[3] For biographical information on the Medici, see Pieraccini, *La stirpe de' Medici di Cafaggiolo*.

[4] *Vite*, 1550, p. 493 (Vasari-Milanesi, III, p. 315).

[5] Vasari's patent error in identifying the central Magus as Giuliano may be due to nothing more than a simple mental lapse (see below).

mo."[6] It is, as a few critics have pointed out, most improbable that the young Magus stands for a man who died at the age of forty-two in 1463, several years before Botticelli can have begun his picture.[7]

Shortly after Vasari published the second edition of the *Lives*, Botticelli's altarpiece was removed from Santa Maria Novella and quickly lost sight of.[8] Since its "rediscovery" in 1848 many critics have commented on the portraits. Of these critics only a few need concern us here. In his monograph on Botticelli of 1893, Heinrich Ulmann, realizing that the central Magus cannot be Giuliano de' Medici, proposed that he represents Piero, the son of Cosimo and the father of Lorenzo and Giuliano (Fig. 3). For Giuliano, Ulmann suggested the dark-haired figure standing directly behind the young Magus (Fig. 39). Lorenzo he consequently identified as the youth with the sword in the extreme left

[6] Vasari-Milanesi, III, pp. 315f.

[7] The identification of the young king with Giovanni seems to have been doubted first by Horne (*Botticelli*, p. 41). When Vasari wrote of the portraits in 1550 he did so as a more or less disinterested observer. But in 1553 he became one of Cosimo I's "iconographers." It was Vasari's job to seek out images of the duke's forebears for use in the portrait galleries then being established and also in his own frescoes in the Palazzo Vecchio. And in this job—especially in the cases of the lesser known Medici, whose images were hard to come by—Vasari might be other than critical in his identifications. One must therefore be on guard against additions to the *Lives* such as the one on Giovanni de' Medici's portrait. Vasari apparently thought that Giovanni was represented in Santa Maria Nuova—presumably in the frescoes of the life of the Virgin in the Cappella Maggiore of the church of Sant'Egidio, now almost entirely destroyed, which Vasari seems to have regarded as a grandiose allegory of the exile and return of Cosimo il Vecchio (see Vasari, *Lo zibaldone*, ed. A. del Vita, p. [260]; and Vasari-Milanesi, II, pp. 676-78). But he nevertheless seems to have decided that Botticelli's altarpiece was the better source for portraits not only of Giovanni but also of his uncle Lorenzo, the brother of Cosimo, who died in 1440 (*Zibaldone*, p. [260]). For their representations of Lorenzo both he and Bronzino made use of the dark-haired man looking out from the group of bystanders at the left (Figs. 19-21). On portrait derivations from Botticelli's altarpiece by Vasari and his contemporaries, see Trapesnikoff, *Die Porträtdarstellungen der Mediceer des XV. Jahrhunderts*, pp. 28, 41f., 74f.; and Langedijk, *De portretten van de Medici tot omstreeks 1600* (diss.), pp. 73-76.

[8] See above, Introduction; and Horne, "Story," pp. 134f. The picture is mentioned by both Raffaello Borghini (*Il Riposo*, p. 352) and Filippo Baldinucci (*Notizie*, III, p. 138), who evidently did not know it first hand but were repeating what they had read in Vasari. Baldinucci in turn is cited on the portraits by Fra Domenico Sandrini (*Notizie*, Appendix II, 2).

foreground (Fig. 31). Ulmann was also responsible for the identification of Sandro Botticelli as the red-haired young man in the right foreground (Fig. 54).[9] In 1903 Jacques Mesnil wrote a short article (which seems for the most part to have gone unnoticed) in which he identified Guasparre dal Lama as the old, pointing man in the group of figures at the right (Fig. 53).[10] In a monograph of 1908, which remains the basic work on Botticelli, Herbert Horne rejected Ulmann's identifications of Giuliano and Lorenzo and also expressed doubts about the identification of Giovanni with the young Magus (Figs. 16-18).[11]

During the seventy years or so that have elapsed since these authors wrote, little of value has been added on the question of the portraits in Botticelli's picture. But the *status quo* has now been challenged in the valuable study on the portraits of the Medici by Karla Langedijk. Aware of the inconsistencies in Vasari (not to mention those in more recent authorities), Professor Langedijk has arrived at an elegant but radical solution: she denies the presence of any of the Medici in the picture. Vasari, she says, in need of images of some of the Medici for the portrait genealogies of that family for which he was responsible, made it all up[12] (although why Vasari should have been hard put to find portraits of Cosimo and Giuliano in 1550 she does not explain).[13] Perhaps Langedijk is right. There is no positive proof that any of the Medici are shown in the altarpiece. However, some forceful points can be brought to bear in defense of the view that they are.

[9] Ulmann, *Botticelli*, pp. 58-60.
[10] Mesnil, "Quelques documents sur Botticelli," p. 94.
[11] Horne, *Botticelli*, pp. 41f.
[12] Langedijk, *Portretten*, pp. 73-76. On Vasari's role as a portrait hunter, see also above, note 7. Other scholars have also communicated to me their skepticism about the presence of the Medici in the picture.
[13] Much as I welcome her fine study, I must here make it clear that I disagree with Langedijk on a number of points. Her argument, in effect that Vasari more or less deliberately put one over on his contemporaries and on posterity, seems in some ways as unhistorical as what she attributes to him (see below, notes 21, 22). Langedijk is certainly right in saying that Vasari is inaccurate on a number of details (as he often is). But the possibility remains that these spurious details may be fabricated around a kernel of truth (as they often are). Properly stated, Langedijk's argument should have been simply that Vasari, here demonstrably inaccurate, is notoriously unreliable on portraits and that his identification of members of the Medici family with the three Magi in Botticelli's altarpiece should therefore be considered a possible legend (whether of Vasari's making or one that had come down to him does not matter), unless it can be proved otherwise.

The chief question at issue is whether or not the Magi in Botticelli's altarpiece are intended as portraits. In fact it seems likely that two of them are. Botticelli painted the Adoration of the Magi at least six times. Of his other surviving paintings of the subject, two are probably earlier and two later than the altarpiece for Guasparre dal Lama.[14] In all of these other pictures the figures of the Magi conform quite closely to Florentine convention, in which they are shown as oriental types (Figs. 12, 14, 60). The first (Balthasar or Melchior) is always bearded and hoary; the second (Melchior or Balthasar) usually a dark, bearded man in his middle years; and the third (Caspar) a very young man. The altarpiece for Guasparre dal Lama is the only one of Botticelli's *Adorations* in which this convention is fully suspended and in which some of the Magi clearly are not stock types. They are beardless and thus not orientals. The tradition of showing the Magi as representatives of the three ages of man is of course respected.

If the Magi in Botticelli's altarpiece are not orientals, what are they? The composition of the painting provides some further clues. In two of the other four surviving paintings of the Adoration by Botticelli, the tondo at London (Fig. 14) and the unfinished panel in the deposit of the Uffizi, the arrangement is similar to that in the altarpiece for Guasparre dal Lama. The Madonna and Child with St. Joseph are set in the center of the picture, at the rear of a clearly demarcated foreground. The Magi are placed in front of the Holy Family and their followers for the most part disposed on either side. The elegance of such an arrangement is that it makes the Magi into a link between the Holy Family and the spectator; they become intercessors. But its inherent difficulties are obvious. If Botticelli wishes his narrative to be "natural" and persuasive, he must conceal the faces

[14] The oblong panel in the National Gallery at London (Fig. 12) appears to be one of Botticelli's earliest works. The tondo in the same museum (Fig. 14) may be a work of the early 1470s. The Mellon panel in the National Gallery of Art at Washington (Fig. 60) appears to date from Botticelli's sojourn in Rome in 1481-82 (on it, see below, Chapter IV, note 21). The unfinished panel in the deposit of the Uffizi (ill.: Salvini, *Botticelli*, II, pl. 70) may have been done in the 1490s. Apparently lost is a painting which the Anonimo Magliabechiano saw at the head of the stairs in front of the Porta della Catena in the Palazzo Vecchio (unless it is identical with the *Adoration* by Cosimo Rosselli; see Salvini, II, p. 70; and below, note 20).

of the Magi. If on the other hand he wants to show the faces, he must compromise the logic of his narrative, since he can no longer face the Magi toward the Holy Family. In the other paintings in which he employs this compositional type, Botticelli follows the former, or narrative course. In a third picture, the Mellon *Adoration* now at Washington (Fig. 60), he sidesteps the issue by placing the Magi on either side of the Holy Family. But for this he must pay, since here the Magi no longer serve as a link between the Holy Family and the spectator. In the altarpiece for Guasparre dal Lama, Botticelli evidently felt it necessary to preserve both the sense of the Magi as intercessors and their faces. Thus two of the Magi must face each other, rather than the Child, and only the position of their bodies tells one that their chief intent is to worship him.

Of the Magi in the altarpiece for Guasparre dal Lama the youngest is clearly a type (Fig. 16); he recurs as the young king in the Mellon *Adoration* (Fig. 60). Although this Magus is a type, Botticelli seems to have gone to remarkable lengths to preserve his face. In fact he appears to be the most important of the three.[15] But the other Magi are not types, and one is struck by the fact that the face of the old Magus is seen in full profile (Figs. 2, 27), and that of the central Magus in the slightest of lost profiles (Fig. 3). To an observer of the Quattrocento such unexpected figurations probably meant portraits (as they certainly did to Vasari).[16]

If the elder Magi in Botticelli's altarpiece are indeed intended as portraits, it follows that they are likely to be members of the Medici. By Botticelli's day the Magi seem often to have been looked upon as the emblematic representatives of the Medici, who

[15] He is Caspar, the namesake of Guasparre dal Lama. With him are associated not only Guasparre but possibly also Lorenzo de' Medici and Botticelli himself (see below).

[16] At the time Botticelli did the altarpiece, most individual portraits in two-dimensional media such as painting or relief sculpture were still almost always done in full or near-profile (Fig. 32). For all its inherent deadness, the profile is that image which best records the immutable aspects of a face. It is the easiest type of portrait in which to catch a likeness, and it is the easiest to remember. The only Florentine painter who seems fully to have broken with the profile before Botticelli's time was Andrea del Castagno in his forceful *Portrait of a Man* in the National Gallery of Art at Washington. (There is, however, some doubt as to whether this painting is a portrait [see Gilbert, review of J. Pope-Hennessy, *The Portrait in the Renaissance*, pp. 281f., and 285, n. 21].)

had adopted the Three Kings as the collective patrons of their family around 1440.[17] It was not long before the association between the Medici and the Magi gave rise to identifications of the family with their patrons in paintings of the Epiphany. In the frescoes of the chapel of the Medici Palace, which were begun in 1459 by Benozzo Gozzoli, the young Magus, Caspar, has their arms (Fig. 22). He is probably intended as the "ideal" typification of the young Lorenzo de' Medici, then about eleven years old.[18] In an *Adoration* by Cosimo Rosselli, roughly contemporary with Botticelli's altarpiece (Figs. 25, 26),[19] the same Magus is associated with one of the bystanders, who may be one of the Medici, through the near-identity of the costumes that the two figures are wearing. Although it is not certain that the bystander in question is intended as one of the Medici, the presence of the family seems clearly implicit in the picture.[20]

[17] On the association between the Medici and the Magi, see Hatfield, "Compagnia," esp. pp. 135-41.

[18] See below.

[19] On the date of the painting, see Lorenzoni, *Cosimo Rosselli*, pp. 44f.

[20] The bystander in question is the dark-haired man facing the viewer, toward the left of the central group. He somewhat resembles Piero de' Medici. On the trappings of the horse at the left of Cosimo Rosselli's picture are what appear to be the devices of Giovanni Rucellai, whose son Bernardo was married to Nannina (Lucrezia) de' Medici, the daughter of Piero, in 1466. As was noted by G. Pudelko ("Studien über Domenico Veneziano," p. 168, n. 3), the painting is based on the tondo by Domenico Veneziano which is now in Berlin. Domenico's tondo may well be identical with a painting of the Adoration listed in the inventory taken of the Medici Palace in 1492 as the work of Pesello: "Uno tondo alto braccia 2 entrovi la storia de' Magi, di mano di Pesello, f. 20" (Müntz, *Collections*, p. 64). Curiously, Cosimo Rosselli's painting, then in the Palazzo Vecchio, was attributed by Vasari to the same painter: "gli fu dalla Signoria di Firenze fatto dipignere una tavola a tempera, quando i Magi offeriscono a Cristo; che fu collocata a mezza scala del Palazzo: per la quale Pesello aquistò gran fama; e massimamente avendo in essa fatto alcuni ritratti, e fra gli altri quello di Donato Acciaiuoli" (Vasari-Milanesi, III, pp. 36f. [see also Milanesi's annotation]; Vasari of course is wrong in thinking that the painting was commissioned by the government of Florence; how it entered the Palazzo Vecchio, in Vasari's day the residence of Duke Cosimo I de' Medici, we do not know). In fact, one of the figures in the group at the left served as the source for later representations of Acciaiuoli (e.g., Allegrini, *Serie di ritratti*, II, fol. 63). A friend of Lorenzo de' Medici's, Acciaiuoli (like Bernardo Rucellai, who probably also figures in the painting) appears to have been quite active in the Compagnia de' Magi (Hatfield, "Compagnia," pp. 124, 129f., 139). Among the other figures in the group at the left it seems possible to make out the features of Carlo de' Medici and also those of two persons, perhaps members of the Capponi family, who are also portrayed in Ghirlandaio's frescoes in the Sassetti

Vasari seems to have been unaware of the association between the Medici and the Magi, one that came to an end when the family was driven from Florence in 1494.[21] What can have led him to believe that some of the Medici are represented in Botticelli's altarpiece? One unfortunately cannot tell. Whatever the basis of the information he gives may have been, Vasari must have been aware of the resemblance between the profile of Botticelli's old Magus (Fig. 27) and that in the medals of Cosimo de' Medici (Figs. 28-30),[22] the earliest of which were done in 1465, the year following that of Cosimo's death.[23] Line for line, the features of Botticelli's old Magus conform to those in the medals. There are to be sure a few differences in their positioning (as in the veins at the temple). And the features in Botticelli's profile are tighter and sharper than those in the medals. But "iconographically" the two faces are the same. There can be no doubt that the profile of Botticelli's old Magus and that in Cosimo de' Medici's medals belong to the same physiognomic *type*. In reflecting upon the two images, Vasari evidently thought Botticelli's the more natural and therefore supposed—unmindful of the hard facts of chronology—that it was taken from the life. Perhaps he even imagined that it was the source for the medals.

Chapel. One may therefore suspect the presence of a Medicean assemblage in the main group as well, although the crudeness of Cosimo Rosselli's figuration seems to make positive identification of the persons represented there impossible.

21 Langedijk (*Portretten*, p. 76) contends that the connection between the Medici and the Compagnia de' Magi was common knowledge in Vasari's day and that this enabled him to gain acceptance among his contemporaries for his identifications of members of the family with the Magi in Botticelli's painting. In fact there is no reason to believe that Vasari or any of his acquaintances had ever heard of the confraternity, which was dissolved immediately after the Medici were expelled, some fifty-six years before Vasari did the first edition of the *Lives* (Hatfield, "Compagnia," p. 140).

22 Langedijk (p. 76) also conjectures that the resemblance between the erect figure standing just behind the young Magus and portraits that Vasari knew of Giuliano de' Medici led Vasari to suppose that members of the Medici are represented in Botticelli's painting. This conjecture hardly seems justified in view of the fact that Vasari states in the first edition of the *Lives* (the error goes uncorrected in the 1568 edition) that Giuliano is portrayed as the second Magus. On Vasari's identification of Giuliano, see below.

23 On Cosimo's medals, which are the basis for all subsequent representations of him, see Hill, *A Corpus of Italian Medals*, nos. 907-910*bis*. See also below.

In fact Botticelli's picture was done well after the earliest of the medals—perhaps by as much as ten years. If there is a direct connection between the two, it was of course one of the medals which served as the source.

Vasari evidently believed quite firmly that Giuliano de' Medici was portrayed by Botticelli as one of the figures in the altarpiece for Guasparre dal Lama.[24] But he is inconsistent in his selection of that figure. For in his medallion of Giuliano in the Palazzo Vecchio, executed after 1556 (Fig. 40), Vasari made use not of the Magus whom he identified as Giuliano in his edition of the Lives of 1550, but of the erect, dark-haired young man toward the front of the group of figures at the right (Fig. 39).[25]

But it appears that Vasari was wrong on both counts and that Ulmann, in proposing for Giuliano the same figure that Vasari had used for his medallion, reversed the more likely positions of Giuliano and his brother.[26] For if they are both portrayed, Giuliano would logically be the youth with the sword at the left,[27] and Lorenzo the erect figure behind the young Magus at the right. Of the young men in question, it should be evident that the one with the sword is the less mature. He has a casual

[24] Had he not been convinced of this, Vasari surely would have used as his source for the medallion of Giuliano in the Palazzo Vecchio either the portrait of him that was in the Guardaroba there, the bust that was used by Bronzino (on both of these, see following note), or the portrait, now destroyed, which Vasari says that Baldovinetti did of him in the frescoes of the Cappella Maggiore of Santa Trinita (Vasari-Milanesi, II, p. 594 [there is no mention of the portraits in Baldovinetti's frescoes in the first edition of the Lives]).

[25] Is Vasari's identification in the first edition of the Lives (which is retained in the edition of 1568) due to a simple mental lapse? Or did Vasari change his mind? If so, he must during the years after 1550 have come to know individual portraits of Giuliano such as the portrait on parchment then in the Guardaroba of the Palazzo Vecchio (on it, see Trapesnikoff, Porträtdarstellungen, p. 76; it seems clear that Vasari knew this portrait [Zibaldone, p. (260)]); or the bust which appears to have been the model for Bronzino's portrait of Giuliano in the series of small portraits of members of the Medici, executed between 1553 and 1568 and now preserved in the Museo Mediceo (Fig. 38; on the portrait and the bust from which it appears to be derived, see Trapesnikoff, pp. 70, 75). Both the bust and the image in Bronzino's portrait somewhat resemble the figure that Vasari gives in the medallion.

[26] Ulmann, Botticelli, pp. 58-60. Ulmann does not mention the derivation by Vasari.

[27] He was thus identified by Müller-Walde (Leonardo, pp. 126f.).

haircut; his forehead is covered with unparted locks of curly black hair.[28] In both dress and pose he is the dandified figure of the *armeggiante*. The figure standing behind the young Magus would, conversely, be Lorenzo. His hair is parted in a more formal manner and he has a more dignified bearing. In both cut and color his costume is the more solemn. Such properties are surely more appropriate to an actual head of state.

Evidence that the young figure with the sword represents Giuliano may be found in Botticelli's posthumous portrait of him (Fig. 33).[29] In fact, it seems that the ultimate source for the posthumous portrait was the figure in the altarpiece (Fig. 31).[30] The positioning and general outlines of the two heads are almost identical. Of course there are differences. In the posthumous portrait the profile has been slightly shifted, so that some of the farther eye becomes visible. But the main differences have to do with personality. The face in the altarpiece is youthful and soft. The eyebrows are high, the nose delicate, the lips curved and full, and the chin, although prominent, gently rounded. In the posthumous portrait the features, stonelike in clarity, are more virile. The eyebrows are lower and straighter, the nose sharper and more aquiline, the lips compressed, and chin more angular.

[28] Botticelli and his contemporaries are quite consistent in representing boys with this haircut. However, it may also be worn by older men. Thus in Ghirlandaio's *Confirmation of the Franciscan Rule* in the Sassetti Chapel, both the young son of Francesco Sassetti and Lorenzo de' Medici (then about thirty-five) have unparted hair (Fig. 41). Lorenzo, however, does have the more formal haircut in a number of his portraits, among them the one in Botticelli's own *Wedding Feast of Nastagio degli Onesti* (Fig. 13).

[29] On this portrait, of which several versions are known, see Langedijk, pp. 21f.; and Salvini, *Botticelli*, 1, pp. 47f.

[30] The source can hardly have been the bust by Verrocchio (Fig. 34), since the bust conveys a rather different personality (on it, see Passavant, *Verrocchio*, pp. 34-36, 183). I cannot accept Langedijk's suggestion that Botticelli made preparatory studies for the portrait during the twenty-four hours or so that elapsed between Giuliano's death in the Pazzi conspiracy and his burial (his funeral services were held on 30 April 1478 but he was buried on 27 April; ASF, Arte dei Medici e Speziali, 246, fol. 34r). Giuliano had been cruelly cut to pieces. Among his wounds was a blow that smashed his skull. The city was in a state of hysteria and the Medici Palace under heavy security. For accounts of the conspiracy and its aftermath, see Poliziano, *Congiura de' Pazzi*, ed. Bonucci, Florence, 1895. The posthumous portrait may, however, owe something to Piero Pollaiuolo's *Portrait of Galeazzo Maria Sforza* in the Uffizi (Fig. 32; the identification is probable but not certain).

Still, the eventual derivation of the posthumous portrait from the figure in the altarpiece remains apparent. Giuliano's downward glance in the posthumous portrait seems adequate indication of it.[31] In the altarpiece the young figure's glance is externally motivated; he is following the actions of the younger Magi. In the posthumous portrait—exactly why one cannot tell, but doubtless in order to capture some quality of the "soul"— Botticelli may have seen fit to emphasize the downward cast of the young figure's eyes rather than change it.

It may even be observed that, in order to do the posthumous portrait, Botticelli needed to refer no farther than to his own altarpiece for Guasparre dal Lama. For all of the salient features in the portrait are to be found in the figures here under discussion: the positioning of the head and shoulders in the youth with the sword at the left (Fig. 31), the haircut and the general cast of the features in the figure standing behind Caspar (Fig. 39), and features such as the nose and chin in the central Magus (Fig. 3).

There is thus a close resemblance in type between the young figure with the sword in Botticelli's altarpiece and Botticelli's own posthumous portrait of Giuliano de' Medici, although here the resemblance is not strictly physiognomical. Once again one may speak of an "iconographic" connection between one of the faces in the altarpiece and an unquestioned image of one of the Medici.

The key portrait figure in the altarpiece is that of the erect young man who stands behind Caspar (Fig. 39). He closely resembles the Giuliano de' Medici of Verrocchio's celebrated bust at Washington (Fig. 34). His resemblance to the Giuliano of Botticelli's posthumous portrait is also apparent. (Only the face in the altarpiece is more jowly and thicker set.) Now, in the posthumous portrait Botticelli represents Giuliano gravely, as a man. He has the more formal haircut, the "hair black and long and pushed away from the forehead at the top," which is mentioned

[31] The downward glance was not a conventional sign of death when Botticelli did the posthumous portrait. If in certain types of individual and double portraits it became so later on, this may well have been as a result of Botticelli's invention. The suggestion that the downward glance was a convention for posthumous portrait images was put forward by Meller ("Cappella," pp. 194-98); and taken up by Langedijk (pp. 21f.).

in Poliziano's description of Giuliano in his account of the Pazzi conspiracy of 26 April 1478, in which Giuliano lost his life.[32] But when did Giuliano attain manhood? The occasion for his initiation into it may have been the sumptuous joust of 28 January 1475, which Poliziano describes in his celebrated *Stanze* (where, in accordance with romantic convention, he makes Giuliano's hair blond).[33] In any case Giuliano clearly had assumed the responsibilities of manhood by the end of that year.[34]

There can be no doubt that the erect figure in Botticelli's altarpiece and the Giuliano de' Medici of the posthumous portrait belong to the same "family" of types. This close iconographic resemblance—as well as the fact that Vasari himself used the face of the erect figure for a portrait of Giuliano—has naturally led to corroboration on the part of most critics of Ulmann's identification of the figure behind Caspar as Giuliano.[35] But the two images do not seem to be portraits of the same *person*. Rather, they must be portraits of *similar* persons at approximately the *same moment in life*. If Botticelli's altarpiece was in fact done during, say, 1473,[36] Lorenzo de' Medici was twenty-four at the time. Giuliano de' Medici was twenty-four when he was murdered in the Cathedral of Florence in April of 1478.[37] In 1473 he was only nineteen or twenty—still on the verge of manhood.

If the erect figure behind Caspar is indeed one of the Medici,

[32] Poliziano, *Della congiura dei Pazzi* (*Coniurationis commentarium*), p. 63: "capillo nigro et promisso atque in occiput a fronte reiecto."

[33] In the *Stanze* Giuliano's hair is mentioned in the passage in which he goes to his mother and is urged by her to let Lorenzo take his place in the joust: "poi tutto al petto si ristringe el figlio / e trattando con man suo chiome bionde / tutto el vagheggia . . ." (Poliziano, *Stanze cominciate per la giostra di Giuliano de' Medici*, II, 13, vv. 6-8 [ed. Pernicone, p. 66]).

[34] On 7 April 1475, as Syndic of the Commune, Giuliano knighted Francesco della Sassetta (Giovanni and Lionardo Morelli, *Chroniche*, p. 191). Giuliano's election to the post of syndic seems to have been an exceptional honor. Normally knights might be created by other knights only. Among the very few other men for whom this rule was suspended was Lorenzo de' Medici, who served as syndic in 1470, when he was already the *de facto* head of state. (See Salvemini, *La dignità cavalleresca nel comune di Firenze*, p. 87.) On 18 August 1475 Giuliano was elected to the Council of the bankers' guild (ASF, Arte del Cambio, 19).

[35] To the best of my knowledge Ulmann's identifications have been followed by all critics who accept the presence of the brothers except for Eve Borsook, who identifies the figures in question as they are identified here (*The Companion Guide to Florence*, p. 146).

[36] On the date of the picture, see above, Chapter I.

[37] Lorenzo was born on 1 January 1448/49, Giuliano on 15 October 1453.

he must be Lorenzo. In Benozzo Gozzoli's frescoes in the chapel of the Medici Palace, Lorenzo appears twice to have been represented under the sign of Caspar: once in person in the young king's following (Fig. 23),[38] and once allegorically as Caspar himself (Fig. 22), in whose person Lorenzo's ideal presence seems to be indicated by the Medici balls in the trappings of the horse and by the spray of foliage which sets off the young king's head.[39] Lorenzo may again be represented by Caspar in the *Adoration* by Cosimo Rosselli (Figs. 25, 26).[40] Out of the broken wall in Botticelli's altarpiece, directly over the young figure's head, there grows a blazonlike shoot of what appears to be laurel (Fig. 4).[41] By way of a pun on his name, laurel (*lauro*) was one of Lorenzo's devices.[42]

[38] In the family group which follows Caspar, Lorenzo appears to be one of the two boys in the second row, just beneath Benozzo's self-portrait (the other presumably is Giuliano). The boys are placed between two clerics who are probably their tutors—perhaps Cristoforo Landino and Gentile de' Becchi. Their portrayal would thus correspond in some ways to that of Lorenzo's sons in Ghirlandaio's fresco of the *Confirmation of the Franciscan Rule* in the Sassetti Chapel. On these portraits, see Warburg, *Gesammelte Schriften*, I, pp. 95-116, 340-47.

[39] This plant is usually identified as laurel (*lauro*), which would assimilate the young king with Lorenzo rather than another member of the family or the family as a whole (see below). The young king also appears to be associated with an orange tree (*l'arancio*) and a lance (*lancia*). For a contrary opinion on the young king's significance, see Gombrich, "The Early Medici as Patrons of Art," p. 49. Gombrich is certainly right in contending that the young king is not a likeness of Lorenzo. Lorenzo's association with Caspar may have been brought about by the circumstance that his birthday falls on the feast day of one of the Magi (usually given as Caspar, but occasionally as Melchior; see the *Acta Sanctorum* under 1 January). Of the three Magi Caspar is usually the first to be invoked; thus the salutation in a letter from the Compagnia de' Magi to another Florentine confraternity: "Guaspar, Baldassar et Melchior" (Hatfield, "Compagnia," p. 148).

[40] See above, especially note 20.

[41] There is, however, a possibility that the plant is myrtle (see above, Chapter II, note 116).

[42] Thus the inscription on one of his medals: "Ut laurus semper Laurenti fama vi rebit" (Hill, *Corpus*, no. 1109). For some early occurrences of the association of laurel with Lorenzo, see Rochon, *La Jeunesse de Laurent de Médicis*, pp. 95, 98. He goes by the name of "Lauro" in Poliziano's *Stanze*. If the laurel in Botticelli's altarpiece is in fact a reference to Lorenzo, it would here have a double symbolic function (on its primary significations, see above, Chapter II), as it also may in the *Portrait of a Woman* ("Laura") attributed to Giorgione at Vienna. The conceit of using "laurel" in a double sense was of course invented by Petrarch. Leonardo, too, seems to have been fond of using a symbol with more than one function in con-

The erect figure in Botticelli's altarpiece may be compared to the only reasonably certain portrait of Lorenzo in Botticelli's oeuvre. This is the figure seated fourth from the right at the right-hand table in the *Wedding Feast of Nastagio degli Onesti*, which was done in 1483 (Fig. 13). The resemblance between the two figures was first noticed by Trifon Trapesnikoff, who, assuming the erect figure in the altarpiece to be Giuliano, identified the seated figure in the *Nastagio degli Onesti* scene also as Giuliano.[43] It has since been shown that the seated figure must be Lorenzo.[44] If one compares the face of the erect figure in the altarpiece to the well-known portrait of Lorenzo in Ghirlandaio's frescoes in the Sassetti Chapel (Fig. 41),[45] which was done perhaps ten years later, one sees that the differences between them are not overly great. In Botticelli's figure there is scant indication of Lorenzo's depressed nose, which is in unflattering evidence in Ghirlandaio's portrait. But its omission may be due to idealization.[46] Nose aside, the face in Botticelli's altarpiece is clearly of the type that served for Ghirlandaio's portrait and for most of Lorenzo's medals (Figs. 35, 37, 43).[47]

---

junction with portrait images. The juniper in his *Ginevra de' Benci* in Washington gives the name of the sitter and doubtless one of her qualities or virtues as well. The ermine in his *Cecilia Gallerani* in Cracow is both an emblem of Ludovico Sforza and, according to Leonardo himself, an "example" of moderation (Möller, "Leonardos Bildnis der Cecilia Gallerani," p. 319).

[43] Trapesnikoff, pp. 73f.

[44] On the revision of the identification, see Langedijk, pp. 20 and 128, n. 78. Lorenzo is seated not far from Antonio Pucci (the father of the groom), with whom he also appears in Ghirlandaio's *Confirmation of the Franciscan Rule* in the Sassetti Chapel (Fig. 41).

[45] On the portrait, see Warburg, *Gesammelte Schriften*, I, pp. 102f., 342f.

[46] The unfortunate nose is also modified in a manuscript illumination of the youthful Lorenzo (Fig. 42; on the illumination, see Langedijk, p. 16); in the romantic engraving of him and Lucrezia Donati (on it, see Warburg, I, pp. 81-87); and in one of Lorenzo's medals (on it, see Hill, *Corpus*, no. 921). In fact, when Botticelli represented Lorenzo in his panel of the *Wedding Feast of Nastagio degli Onesti*, he made Lorenzo's nose somewhat aquiline.

[47] On the medals, see Hill, nos. 915-16, 921, 926, 987-88. One of the bystanders in Botticelli's tondo of the *Adoration* at London might also be Lorenzo. The painting may have been done for Antonio Pucci, one of Lorenzo's closest supporters (Davies, *The Earlier Italian Schools*, p. 102), along with whom Lorenzo appears in two other pictures (see above, note 44). Pucci's arms, a Moor's head, were those of one of the Magi. The bystander in question, seen in strict profile and wearing a feather in his hat (the

The portrait identity of the central Magus in Botticelli's altar-piece (Fig. 3) is quite problematical. In his face, too, there is a close physiognomic similarity to that in the posthumous portrait of Giuliano de' Medici (Fig. 33). The character of his profile is quite the same as Giuliano's there. Now, the features of the central Magus may be nothing more than a cross of those of the old Magus (Fig. 27) with those of the erect figure behind Caspar (Fig. 39)—just as those of Giuliano in the posthumous portrait may be nothing more than a conflation of the figures of the youth with the sword, the figure behind Caspar, and the central Magus. The hybrid nature of a number of Botticelli's faces should by now be apparent. From a few basic facial types he might generate a whole "family" of others.

If Botticelli was in fact proceeding in this way when he painted the face of the central Magus, it must be admitted that the result is not very close in appearance to the known images of the person who must here have been intended. If the painting contains portraits of the Medici, it is quite clear that the old Magus represents Cosimo (Fig. 27); the erect figure behind Caspar, Lorenzo (Fig. 39); and the youth with the sword, Giuliano (Fig. 31)—in other words the founder of the family's hegemony in Florence, who was dead, and his two grandsons, who were living. The Magi traditionally stand for the ages of man. Hence the central Magus might be expected to represent one of the deceased members of the generation between Cosimo's and Lorenzo's. This should mean either Piero or Giovanni de' Medici, the sons of Cosimo.[48] Of the two, Piero would seem by far the more likely subject, since he, the elder, was Cosimo's political heir and also the father of Lorenzo and Giuliano.[49]

But if one compares the profile of the central Magus (Fig. 3) to such surviving portraits of Piero as the profile in the frescoes by Benozzo Gozzoli (Fig. 49) or the bust by Mino da Fiesole

---

feather is often found as a Medici emblem), occurs in the uppermost group of onlookers to the left of the Holy Family (Fig. 15). His features have a marked resemblance to those in some of Lorenzo's medals (Fig. 43).

[48] Piero died in 1469, Giovanni in 1463. Cosimo's brother Lorenzo had one son, Pierfrancesco, who was born in 1430 and died in 1476; we have no sure knowledge of his appearance.

[49] Ulmann's identification of the central Magus as Piero (Botticelli, p. 58) has been followed by nearly all critics who accept the presence of the Medici in Botticelli's altarpiece.

(Fig. 47),[50] one finds that the resemblance is slight.[51] The figure of the central Magus can however be related to the images of one of Cosimo's offspring. This is Carlo, the illegitimate son, who spent the years from 1460 until his death in 1492 as provost of the Duomo of Prato. It is probably Carlo's features that are known to us from a striking portrait by Andrea Mantegna, perhaps of 1466 (Fig. 48).[52] He appears also to have been represented in profile by Benozzo Gozzoli as the figure just behind that of Piero in the frescoes of the Medici Palace (Fig. 46).[53] Here the set of the eyes, nose, mouth, and chin seems remarkably close to that of the central Magus in Botticelli's picture.

What is one to make of such a resemblance? It does not seem likely that Botticelli intended to convey here the presence of Carlo de' Medici, historically a rather obscure figure who was hardly known in Florence. Is the resemblance purely fortuitous? Did Botticelli draw upon the features of Cosimo's only living son in order to represent one who was dead? Or is it possible that a "reconstruction" by Botticelli of a member of the Medici of the generation between Cosimo's and Lorenzo's indeed happened to turn out looking like one of them (even if it was the wrong one)? There is no way one can tell. If there are members of the Medici in Botticelli's altarpiece, it is probable that the

[50] Piero's medal, which is known in only two examples, is of such poor craftsmanship that it seems pointless to consider it as a record of Piero's actual appearance. The medal, along with that of Giovanni, with which it forms a pair, may have been destined for the Sforza at Milan, where one of the examples is now preserved. On it, see Hill, *Corpus*, no. 908.

[51] One wonders, therefore, whether the central Magus might not represent Giovanni de' Medici, whom Vasari identified as the "third king." Unfortunately, the only sure portrait we possess of Giovanni is his medal (Fig. 44). The medal, of which only two examples are known, was evidently designed as a pendant to Piero's (see preceding note). On it, see Hill, no. 907. Like Piero's, Giovanni's medal is so crude in execution that it seems unwise to draw conclusions from it about Giovanni's appearance. All that it really tells us about Giovanni is that he probably was balding. As Langedijk shows (*Portretten*, pp. 11f.), there is no firm evidence that the well-known bust by Mino da Fiesole in the Bargello (Fig. 45) represents Giovanni. I am not convinced by her arguments in favor of retaining the identification.

[52] The identification of Carlo's portrait was made on the basis of a sixteenth-century woodcut derived from it, by Schaeffer ("Ein Medicäer-Bildnis von Mantegna"). See also Gilbert's review of Pope-Hennessy, p. 282, n. 5; and Langedijk, *Portretten*, p. 16.

[53] Often identified as Giovanni, that figure, if the identification of Mantegna's portrait is correct, clearly represents Carlo.

central Magus is one of them, since the positioning of his head and the character of his profile are strong indications that a portrait was intended. In that case the likelihood remains that the figure represents Piero.

In matters of portrait identifications in Florentine Quattrocento paintings one is up against formidable difficulties. (This was as true in Vasari's day as it is now.) The artist of the Quattrocento did not always feel bound to preserve his subject's likeness.[54] One occasionally comes across images that are pure stereotypes, yet one knows from inscriptions and other identificatory conventions that they were intended as portraits. It more often happens that the artist has taken the actual appearance of his subject into account but also made adjustments in his image in order to convey qualities such as the subject's personality, character, status, emotions, and so on. The range of these adjustments may in some instances be so great that different portraits of the same man seem to represent entirely different persons.[55]

In producing an "adjusted" portrait, Quattrocento artists might work in one of two manners. The first was to start with the closest obtainable likeness (in some cases a cast was taken of the subject's face) and work from there to a more generalized image. The other was to begin with a stock vocabulary of feature types and subtypes, and by judicious combination of these work toward an approximation of the subject's appearance. Of the two procedures Botticelli clearly preferred the second. In fact he seems to have been thoroughly type-bound throughout his career. Strictly speaking, there are no likenesses in Botticelli's painting. There are only types.

[54] On the art of portraiture during the Quattrocento, see especially Meller, "Cappella"; Hatfield, "Five Early Renaissance Portraits"; Pope-Hennessy, *The Portrait in the Renaissance*; and Gilbert's review of Pope-Hennessy.

[55] Something approaching this range of variation obtains among the known portraits of Lorenzo de' Medici (Figs. 13, 22, 23, 35, 37, 41-43). But considerably more extreme cases can be demonstrated; e.g., in the portraits of Bartolommeo Colleoni, which include the celebrated equestrian monument by Verrocchio at Venice, a fresco at Bergamo (ill.: *Storia di Milano*, VII, p. 233), and a medal (Hill, *Corpus*, no. 412). See also the portraits of Ludovico Gonzaga illustrated in Lavin, "Piero della Francesca's Flagellation," figs. 23-29.

In painting, as in any other art, the type is the basic unit in a conventional system of communication. What, then, did Botticelli mean to convey in types such as the old Magus, the central Magus, the youth with the sword, and the erect figure behind Caspar? Is this his iconography of the Medici? There are good reasons for believing that it is. The head of the old Magus (Fig. 27) is clearly of the type that served for portraits of Cosimo de' Medici.[56] But would Florentines have been prepared to recognize a conventional image of Cosimo? In fact, it seems that they would (although they might not necessarily have been able to recognize his likeness). For Cosimo, along with Dante, Petrarch, and a handful of others, was by the 1470s one of the few Florentine laymen who had an "iconography" with which many Florentines must have been familiar. In March 1465, about seven months after his death, it was decreed that he should henceforth be called by the title of *Pater patriae*. A public monument commemorating this decree was ordered to be built in memory of his services to the Commune, as evidence of its gratitude and in order that posterity might be reminded of Cosimo's example.[57] Within a short time a large number of medals was issued, all bearing the inscription, *Pater patriae* (Figs. 29, 30).[58] They have served as the basis for all subsequent representations of Cosimo de' Medici.

In Botticelli's day Piero de' Medici had no "iconography" that we know of. There was no general issue of his medals,[59] and

[56] That, however, is not its only use. It served also for representations of the Roman emperor Galba (I owe this information to E. H. Gombrich) and the Bergamese *condottiere* Colleoni (ill.: *Storia di Milano*, VII, p. 233; for bringing this portrait to my attention I am indebted to David Brown).

[57] ASF, Consigli Maggiori, Provvisioni, Registri, 155, fols. 261v-262v (15 March 1464/65): "prefactus vir clarissimus Cosmus Johannis filius Medix, cum summa, atque amplissima beneficia in rem publicam Florentinam bello et pace contulerit . . . deinceps per omne tempus pro eius huiusmodi maximis virtutibus amplissimisque in patriam meritis PATER PATRIAE NUNCUPATUR. . . . Et insuper decem viri quibus huius clarissimi viri honorandi cura per provisionem obtentam per consilia opportuna civitatis Florentie de mense Augusti proxime decursi, comissa sunt, possint ac teneantur et debeant cum effectu providere, ut huiussce decreti monumentum fiat quocunque modo et in quocunque loco et tempore eis utilius visum fuerit, ad perpetuam suorum erga patriam meritorum memoriam grateque patrie testimonium. Ac posterorum exemplum."

[58] On Cosimo's medals, see Hill, *Corpus*, nos. 907-910*bis*. We do not know by whom they were issued.

[59] On the only known medal of Piero, see above, note 50.

none of his other portraits of which we know was to be seen
in a public location. During the later part of his life, moreover,
he may never have appeared in public.[60] But his sons, Lorenzo
and Giuliano, had indeed been seen in public on a number of
festive occasions of which they were the centers of attraction.[61]
It is doubtful whether their medals were abroad in large numbers
at the time when Botticelli did the altarpiece.[62] But it is at least
certain that Lorenzo and Giuliano did have an "iconography"
during the 1470s.[63] All portraits of them from about 1465 to 1478
are rather standardized images of a type of *jeunesse dorée*.[64] To
this category belong the youth with the sword and the erect
figure behind Caspar in Botticelli's altarpiece.

   Thus three of the four figures under discussion in Botticelli's
altarpiece have clear "iconographic" links to Cosimo, Lorenzo,
and Giuliano de' Medici. The fourth, the central Magus, although
closely related to the other three figures in appearance, has only
a tenuous iconographic connection with Piero de' Medici, in
that he somewhat resembles the known images of Piero's illegitimate brother (Figs. 3, 46, 48) and has certain physiognomical
similarities to Piero's younger son as he appears in the posthumous
portrait by Botticelli himself (Fig. 33). But because of Piero's
lack of public exposure, there may have been little sense in re-
cording his actual appearance—if indeed Botticelli knew what it
was. Hence perhaps Botticelli's decision to cross the faces of the
old Magus and the erect figure behind Caspar for that of his
central Magus, drawing on familiar images of the Medici in
order to convey the presence of one whose image was as yet

   [60] I know of no important public appearance by Piero after his tenure
of the office of *gonfaloniere* in January and February 1461. A sickly man,
he seems—even during moments of crisis or the greatest of state occasions—
to have directed from his town palace or his villas in the outlying countryside. His features may have been as much a mystery to most Florentines
as those of Duke Filippo Visconti to the Milanese, who are said to have
flocked to Visconti's bier, when he died in 1447, in order to find out what
he looked like.
   [61] On their public appearances, see Rochon, *Jeunesse, passim.*
   [62] On the medals of the brothers, see Hill, nos. 915-16, 921, 926, 986-88,
1030.
   [63] On the portraits of the brothers prior to 1480, see Trapesnikoff, *Porträtdarstellungen*, pp. 44-56, 68-73; and Langedijk, *Portretten*, pp. 15-26.
   [64] See also the engraving of Lorenzo and Lucrezia Donati, probably of
about 1466 (discussed in Warburg, *Gesammelte Schriften*, I, pp. 81-87);
and the putative bust of Lorenzo in the Museum of Fine Arts at Boston
(Passavant, *Verrocchio*, pp. 35, 203f.).

unfamiliar. It is in any case the cumulative presence of four figures in Botticelli's altarpiece, all in positions of importance and
all related in type to conventional images of the Medici, that
inclines one to believe that the Medici are in fact represented.
However confused he may have been, Vasari, it seems, had some
notion of what he was talking about.[65]

What is one to make of the possible fact of the presence in Botticelli's altarpiece of the Medici in the guise of Magi or their
immediate followers? The Medici, it is thought with good reason, were quite prudent. They avoided where possible most acts
which might give offense, especially those which might allude to
the potential "arrogance" of their condition.[66] But in Botticelli's

[65] One might take the presence of the Medici in Botticelli's altarpiece
as reasonably sure were it not for our uncertainty on a closely related
question. For, their presence or absence may be contingent upon the date
of the picture. We have good grounds for believing that Botticelli's altarpiece was painted in or before 1475 (see above, Chapter 1). However,
the evidence leaves some room for doubt. Now, Giuliano de' Medici is
not likely to have been represented after 1475 with a haircut such as that
of the youth with the sword (Fig. 31). His identification with that figure
is thus disproved if a date of after 1475 is established for Botticelli's picture.
And if Giuliano's identification with the youth with the sword is disproved,
that of Lorenzo with the figure behind Caspar becomes doubtful (Fig. 39),
and, with it, that of Piero with the central Magus (Fig. 3). The resemblance in type between the profile of the old Magus and that in the medals
of Cosimo de' Medici (Figs. 27-30) is not in itself sufficient to prove the
presence of the Medici in Botticelli's altarpiece. A "domino" relationship
exists among the four figures. If one of the identifications falls, so may the
rest. And one of them, that of Giuliano with the youth with the sword,
is fully exposed to considerations of chronology. Thus if Botticelli's altarpiece was done in or before 1475, there probably are at least four members
of the Medici in the picture. If it was done after that date, there may only
be two (in the old Magus and the figure behind Caspar—who might now
be either Lorenzo or Giuliano) or there may be none at all.

[66] In the chapel of their palace there is ample reference to their elevated
status (Figs. 22-24). I am referring to the princely opulence of the chapel,
which room appears to have been unique in Florence, and to the fact that
in Benozzo's frescoes Piero de' Medici and his household are represented
on horseback (a number of other Florentine citizens are not) along with
what appear to be two of the leading lords of Italy (on them, see Mesnil,
"Sigismondo Malatesta e Galeazzo Maria Sforza in un affresco del Gozzoli"). But the chapel of the Medici Palace was the family's private affair.
On the outside their palace shifts to a lower key; it is still implicitly
"arrogant," but in a more respectful way (on how it was perceived at the
time it was built, see Hatfield, "Some Unknown Descriptions of the Medici
Palace in 1459").

altarpiece the Medici may appear in a way that might indeed have grated upon the sensibilities of those Florentines who believed in upholding the traditions of Florentine republicanism— however fictitious they may have become. The Magi were near-saints who traditionally were thought of as kings (although the elder Magi need not be kings in Botticelli's picture).[67] To show the Medici as Magi would seem to have been tantamount to dangling a set of dangerous implications before the public. How might it have been permissible?

Any attempt to explain the possible presence of the Medici in Botticelli's altarpiece should start with Guasparre dal Lama. The Magi were of course his patrons. If in the altarpiece the elder of them are in fact Cosimo and Piero de' Medici, the two deceased banker-statesmen would therefore be intended as patrons as well. Now of the three Magi, the most important from Guasparre's point of view was Caspar; Caspar was Guasparre's namesake. In the altarpiece he is the only Magus who clearly is nothing more than a simple type. But he is closely associated with the erect figure (who is set between him and Guasparre) and who may represent Lorenzo de' Medici. Lorenzo would thus be intended as Guasparre's immediate patron. And perhaps he really was. Or if not, Guasparre had every reason to wish that Lorenzo might become benevolently disposed toward him. Guasparre was a man on the make, and one rarely rose far on the ladder of Florentine society without approval from the Medici Palace. How Lorenzo's patronage might have operated in Guasparre's case we cannot tell. There are thousands of surviving letters to the Medici expressing gratitude for past favors or requesting new ones. However, none from Guasparre is among them.[68] Thus we can hardly hope to know precisely what, if anything, transpired between Guasparre dal Lama and Lorenzo de' Medici.

But there can hardly be much doubt that Lorenzo and Guasparre were acquainted. As the leading bankers of Florence the Medici had a dominant role in the Arte del Cambio, where Guasparre seems to have found and lost his greatest opportu-

[67] It may here be observed that only Caspar has what is clearly a crown. The elder Magi have hats similar to those worn or held by some of the bystanders.

[68] Most of the letters of course are from persons who lived outside Florence or were temporarily absent from the city. Florentines in residence might more fruitfully go in person to the Medici Palace.

nity.[69] Guasparre must also have been acquainted with Lorenzo in one or more of the Florentine lay confraternities. One confraternity to which Guasparre belonged, the Compagnia di Gesù Pellegrino, was joined by Lorenzo on 14 September 1466—evidently for political reasons.[70] The other confraternity of which Guasparre is known to have been a member, the Compagnia di San Piero Martire, was dedicated to the patron saint of Piero de' Medici.[71] There was also the confraternity dedicated to Guasparre's patrons, the Compagnia de' Magi.[72] From about 1436 the Medici took great interest in the Compagnia de' Magi, to which they made generous contributions.[73] During the late 1460s and the 1470s Lorenzo de' Medici seems to have given a great deal of his attention to the confraternity.[74] Unfortunately, none of its records is known, and so there is no way of telling whether Guasparre dal Lama belonged to it. A "son of the holy Magi" by name, he certainly must have wanted to, if only for the prestige.

If the Medici are present in Botticelli's painting, it seems clear that their presence is at least partially due to tribute or to an as yet unfulfilled wish on the part of Guasparre dal Lama. What little we know of Guasparre's character leads one to suspect that he would have expected to gain by having them included in his altarpiece. Whether for favors already received or for services hoped for in the future, he might thus glorify them and, in so doing, attract their attention. Guasparre was an operator, and

[69] In the guild's deliberations for these years, the Medici are once called "our great benefactors" (ASF, Arte del Cambio, 19, under 30 April 1471). They and the other members of their bank were regularly among the guild's consuls and councilors. The Medici Bank is always first on the lists of its member companies.

[70] *Libro di memorie* of that confraternity (BNC, Magl., VIII, 1282), fol. 103v.

[71] It seems possible that Piero belonged to this confraternity. His name does not occur among the somewhat fragmentary remains of its records. However, it is known that the Dominican Order was greatly indebted to Piero (see below) and that he contributed generously toward the veneration of St. Peter Martyr at Milan (Hatfield, "Compagnia," p. 137, n. 145).

[72] On this confraternity, see Hatfield, "Compagnia." It convened in the monastery of San Marco. San Marco is where the second of Guasparre's wills was drawn up (the witnesses were all friars of the monastery). In the will there is a provision for Masses of St. Gregory to be said at San Marco for Guasparre's soul. (See Appendix 1, 3.)

[73] Hatfield, "Compagnia," esp. pp. 135-37.

[74] *Ibid.*, esp. pp. 122-27.

we have witnessed more than one occasion on which he seems to have shown little respect for decorum. This brings us to an important point: if the picture was offensive to republican sentiment, the fault could not be laid to the Medici. Any role they might have had in its ideation would have been passive. (Had it been otherwise they would, one might think, have provided Botticelli with a better image of Piero for the figure of the central Magus.) If Guasparre dal Lama wanted to include some of the Medici in his altarpiece, that was Guasparre's affair. Needless to say, he, too, stands to gain in stature by association with persons of their position.

But would the initiative for the inclusion of the Medici necessarily have come from Guasparre? There was after all another person who stood to gain from catching the notice of the powerful family. This was the painter, Sandro Botticelli, who according to Vasari was catapulted to fame by Guasparre's altarpiece. Vasari claims that the altarpiece brought Botticelli the attention of Sixtus IV. But as Herbert Horne has observed, if Botticelli intended the picture as a demonstration piece, it was not Sixtus IV but the Medici toward whom he must have been making his pitch.[75] And in fact Botticelli began to receive commissions from the Medici in the mid-1470s.[76]

---

[75] "Story," pp. 143f.

[76] For the joust of Giuliano de' Medici, held on 28 January 1475, Botticelli did a standard representing Pallas Athena; the standard was still kept in the Medici Palace in 1492 (on it, see Poggi, "La Giostra Medicea del 1475 e la 'Pallade' del Botticelli"; and Warburg, Gesammelte Schriften, I, 23-25, 312). There followed in 1478 the posthumous portrait of Giuliano. From around the same year is the Primavera, probably commissioned by Lorenzo di Pierfrancesco, the second cousin of Lorenzo and Giuliano di Piero. The Portrait of a Man Holding a Medal of Cosimo de' Medici in the Uffizi (Fig. 28), perhaps representing one of the Medici, may also have been done during the 1470s. The friars of Santa Maria Novella could hardly have objected to the inclusion of portraits of the Medici in the altarpiece for Guasparre dal Lama. Fra Giovanni di Carlo produced a work defending Cosimo and his family against the attacks of Filelfo and giving rather slanted accounts of the conspiracy against Piero de' Medici, the war that followed upon it, and Lorenzo's war against Sixtus IV (Libri de temporibus suis [Rome, Biblioteca Apostolica Vaticana, Vat. Lat. 5878], 1480-82). Fra Domenico da Corella, perhaps the most eminent maestro of the monastery at the time (he barely missed becoming general of the Dominican Order), dedicated his Theotocon to Piero de' Medici (Orlandi, Necrologio, II, pp. 310-12; the dedication is printed in Bandini, Catalogus codicum Latinorum, II, cols. 137f.). The work contains eulogistic descriptions of all Florentine churches then consecrated to Mary

If the Medici are portrayed in the altarpiece for Guasparre dal Lama, there evidently was an element of flattery in back of the idea to have them included. Some of the Florentines might have looked upon their association with Magi as an arrogant conceit. But others might have seen it as an ingenious addition to the theme of Medicean devotion to God and the Church.[77] For if present the Medici are, after all, performing a laudable act.

But if such a representation might have been bold, it would not have been without ties to convention. There were both pictorial and literary precedents for what appears to have transpired in Botticelli's altarpiece. The altarpiece for Guasparre dal Lama may be the first Florentine picture of the Adoration in which public figures are recognizable as Magi. But it would not be alone in the Quattrocento. A tondo by Ghirlandaio (Fig. 61) and the altarpiece that Filippino Lippi completed in 1496 for the monastery of San Donato a Scopeto (Fig. 62) both appear to contain at least one Magus with the features of an actual person.[78] In the north the same step was taken somewhat earlier. The young Magus in the Columba Altarpiece by Roger van der Weyden is thought to have the features of Charles the Bold, Duke of Burgundy (Fig. 59).[79] Although this may not be so, there is no doubt

---

(and a few others that were not), among which a number of Medicean foundations are praised with particular fervor (the third and fourth books, in which the descriptions are found, are published in *Deliciae eruditorum*, ed. G. Lami, Florence, 1742, XII [XIII], pp. 49-116). The Dominicans seem to have been greatly indebted to Piero. After he had sent an offering to the Dominican chapter general in Rome, it was ordered that every Dominican priest say a Mass for his soul. In 1470, the year after Piero's death, the chapter general at Avignon put him on the list of those for whom the entire Order was required to do suffrage (Orlandi, II, p. 310).

[77] On that theme, see Gombrich, "Early Medici."

[78] The elderly Magus looking over his shoulder in Ghirlandaio's tondo of 1487, now in the Uffizi, is clearly identical with one of the onlookers in Ghirlandaio's fresco of the *Calling of the First Apostles* in the Sistine Chapel. That man has been identified as John Argyropulos (c. 1410-c. 1492) by Steinmann (*Die sixtinische Kapelle*, I, pp. 385f.). The face of the old Magus in Filippino's altarpiece, also in the Uffizi, is based on what appears to be a portrait drawing (Scharf, *Filippino Lippi*, p. 128, no. 288, fig. 168). This drawing may have been combined with a figure study for an old Magus (*ibid.*, no. 279, fig. 171) to produce the bearded image that one sees in the altarpiece. According to Vasari, the younger Magi in Filippino's painting represent Giovanni di Pierfrancesco de' Medici and his brother Pierfrancesco [*sic*] (Vasari-Milanesi, III, p. 473).

[79] In a paper given at the College Art Association meeting at Boston on 31 January 1969, Anne Schultz proposed a dating in the early 1450s for the

that the first Magus in the miniature of the *Adoration* from the Book of Hours which Jean Fouquet did for Etienne Chevalier, probably during the 1450s, is Charles VII of France (Fig. 51).[80]

These equations of actual rulers with Biblical figures followed the rules of the "type" and the devotional "imitation." The king of France was a suitable *typus* or *figura* of one of the Three Kings. He customarily made oblations of gold, frankincense, and myrrh at the altar on Epiphany Day.[81] This act pointed up the mystical affinity that was believed to make him "typical" of the Biblical figures.[82] His *imitatio* was intended as the manifestation of those inward qualities of devotion which made him Magi-like. This was also true of Duke Charles the Bold, who engaged in similar ceremonies.

In the frescoes by Benozzo Gozzoli in the chapel of the Medici Palace, the young king appears to stand allegorically for the eleven-year-old Lorenzo de' Medici (Fig. 22), and more tenuous analogies seem to exist between the elder Magi and the figures

Columba Altarpiece. If she is correct, it is unlikely that the young Magus represents Charles the Bold. On the identification, see Panofsky, *Early Netherlandish Painting*, p. 286; but see also Kehrer, *Drei Könige*, II, p. 236, n. 1.

[80] On the miniature, see Ring, *A Century of French Painting*, p. 212 (Fouquet's own portrait of Charles VII, now in the Louvre, is illustrated by Ring on pl. 69). Other paintings which are believed on good grounds to contain portraits of actual persons as Magi include an *Adoration* attributed to Marco Cardisco (c. 1486-1546) in the Museo di San Martino at Naples, in which Robert of Sicily and Charles of Calabria appear to be represented (Doria, *Il Museo e la Certosa di S. Martino*, p. 30); the *Adoration* by Gossaert at Castle Howard, one of the kings in which is thought to be Philip of Burgundy (Brockwell, *The "Adoration of the Magi" by Jan Mabuse*, p. 2 and app. A, p. 1); an altarpiece in the style of Michael Wolgemut in the Germanisches Nationalmuseum at Nuremberg, in which one of the Magi appears to have the profile of the Kanonikus Schönborn (Kehrer, II, p. 253); and an *Adoration* by the Master of the Aachen Altarpiece, now at Mehlem, in which one of the Magi is the subject of the well-known *Man with a Carnation* at Berlin, once attributed to Jan van Eyck (Kehrer, II, pp. 279f.; Nilgen, "Epiphany," p. 316). To leaf through the last sixty-five pages or so of Kehrer's second volume should convince one that the portrayal of actual persons as Magi was quite common during the last decades of the fifteenth century and the first decades of the sixteenth—that is, just on the eve of the Reformation.

[81] On these oblations, see Martène, *De antiquis Ecclesiae ritibus*, III, p. 43; and Kehrer, I, p. 52.

[82] "All the kings of the earth shall adore him . . ." (Psalm 71:11, which forms part of the Offertory chant for the Mass of the Epiphany).

of Piero and Cosimo.[83] These assimilations of course are a family
affair, as is not the case in the northern examples.

In the frescoes of the Medici Palace identity seems to have
been established in terms of *imitatio* only. We know that the
Medici actually took part in the Festa de' Magi, the pageant that
was performed from time to time by the Compagnia de' Magi.[84]
Perhaps they even rode as kings. The Festa de' Magi was most
elaborate. Its participants were done up in finery imagined to
represent the orient, but which in fact seems largely to have been
modelled upon that of the European courts of the time.[85] All of
this may have afforded a good deal of vicarious gratification, but
it cannot have been taken too seriously. The Magi were perceived as the representatives of an exotic dream world, far from
the stern realities of Florentine public life.[86]

But the devotion of the Medici toward the Three Kings was
by no means a fiction, and their imitation of them not just out-
ward.[87] The sense of spiritual affinity which the family seems to
have had toward its patrons made possible the kinds of assimilation between them that one sees in Benozzo Gozzoli's frescoes
(Figs. 22-24). It is apparent that the esthetic gap between the
family and its patrons was still very wide. It is openly bridged
in the case of the very young only, whose innocence must have
exempted them from the dictates of decorum. Even so, the person of Lorenzo is split in two: he appears once as he was (Fig.
23), and once in the guise of the conventional boy-king (Fig.
22).[88] The connection between the elder Medici and their heaven-
ly counterparts is only hinted at. The Medici were not "types" of
the Three Kings. The family was one thing and the Magi an-

---

[83] Thus Piero, who represents the second "age" of Cosimo's family, is
riding a white horse, as does the central Magus. Cosimo is riding a mule;
the eldest Magus rides an ass or mule (for Cosimo's identification, which I
find probable, see Gombrich, "Early Medici," pp. 49f.). Other such associa-
tions may occur in the *Adoration* by Cosimo Rosselli, evidently commissioned by the Rucellai, who were related to the Medici by marriage (Figs.
25, 26). Here the young king again may allegorically represent Lorenzo de'
Medici. (See above, note 20.)
[84] Hatfield, "Compagnia," p. 136.
[85] On the pageant, see Hatfield, pp. 108-19.
[86] *Ibid.*, pp. 119-21, 141-44.
[87] *Ibid.*, pp. 135-41.
[88] See above, p. 79.

other. Thus there was no way for Benozzo to bring them together.[89]

In order for the Medici to become plausible "types" of the Magi,
some fundamental changes were needed. The Medici had to be
exalted ideologically and the Magi to become psychically more
accessible. The exaltation of the Medici was already underway
by the 1450s in the eulogies and other epideiktic works that began
to pour from the pens of the Florentine humanists, poets, and
clergy.[90] Many of these are known; however, the most syco-
phantic of all has thus far received slight attention. It is a poem,
written in 1459 by an unknown author,[91] which contains the
following verses, spoken by the personification of Florence, about
Cosimo de' Medici:

I would say that nature has done badly;
  if only she could take back
  having created Cosimo a mortal!
For, so noble a creature,
  worthy of such virtue and grace and glory,
  would like to be immortal and pure.
O how glorious and triumphant my standard
  then would be, up till the day
  when the judgment shall come of the good and the guilty!
But leaving wishes behind, let me return to reason:
  I say that God has done all things with justice
  and zeal throughout the whole universe;
And that when Cosimo is in heaven,
  no less will he work for my glory
  than he has done or may do on earth's surface.

[89] In Cosimo Rosselli's painting (Figs. 25, 26) the dual images appear
to have been dropped. But an esthetic barrier between earth and heaven
remains. The young king may represent Lorenzo, but he cannot be said
to have Lorenzo's features. His portrait identity can be deduced only on
the basis of foreknowledge (see above, esp. note 20).

[90] On these works see Brown, "The Humanist Portrait of Cosimo de'
Medici."

[91] *Terze rime in lode di Cosimo de' Medici e de' figli e dell'honoranza
fatta l'anno 1458* [*sic*] *al figlio del duca di Milano et al papa nella loro
venuta a Firenze* (BNC, Magl., VII, 1121). On the poem see Hatfield,
"Some Unknown Descriptions," p. 233.

And he shall act before Jove as my advocate,
and in every talent each can do more,
the nearer he is to God and still more blessed.[92]

The already saintly Cosimo shall be an intercessor before God,
just as he may be for Guasparre dal Lama—to whom the poet
by no means yields in bad taste. Elsewhere in the poem the poet
loses all sense of measure and draws a prolix set of analogies between Cosimo and both Christ and God the Father.[93] There are
also verses on Piero, which are only slightly more restrained.[94]

This sort of thing was for private consumption only and can
hardly have been taken very seriously. But it is a different matter
when Marsilio Ficino, punning on the word "cosmos," writes
of Cosimo de' Medici that God formed him "upon the model of
the world (*ad ideam mundi*)."[95] Although Ficino surely did not
have it in mind to do so, he helped with his pun to forge a conceptual link between Cosimo and the Magi. For as we have seen,
the Magi represent the world.[96] In a more earnest vein Ficino
says that the models of virtue which Plato had shown him were

---

[92] Fol. 11v:
　　Io direi ch'ella avesse fatto male;
　　　si potesse riprender la natura
　　　ad aver fatto Chosimo mortale!
　　Però ch'una sì nobil creatura,
　　(Fol. 12r):
　　　di tal virtù et grazia et gloria dengnia,
　　　esser vorrebbe et inmortale et pura.
　　O quanta gloriosa la mia insengnia
　　　et triunfal sarebbe insino al giorno
　　　che 'l giudicio de' buoni et de' rei vengnia!
　　Ma lasciando la voglia, a rragion torno;
　　　dicho che 'l tutto chon giustizia et zelo
　　　à fatto Iddio per l'universo intorno,
　　Et che quando chostui sarà nel cielo,
　　　non men per la mia gloria arà oprato
　　　ch'à fatto o faccia in sul terreste telo.
　　Et fia dinanzi a Giove il mio avochato,
　　　et in ongni fachultà ciaschun più può
　　　quant'è più presso a Iddio et più beato.

[93] Fols. 9v-10v.
[94] Fols. 26v-27r, 84r-v.
[95] Marsilio Ficino, letter to Lorenzo de' Medici [August 1464], in *Opera
omnia*, I, p. 649: "Vale, et sicut Deus Cosmum ad ideam mundi formavit,
ita te ipse quemadmodum coepisti, ad ideam Cosmi figura."
[96] Above, Chapter II, pp. 55-60.

realized by Cosimo in everyday life.[97] For Ficino, as has been
remarked,[98] this is tantamount to calling Cosimo a saint. Ficino
was not alone in exalting Cosimo in philosophic terms. For John
Argyropulos he was an Aristotelian philosopher-ruler, and for
Bartolommeo Scala, the exemplar of divine fortitude and wis-
dom.[99] Cosimo has here come far from the role of powerful but
ordinary citizen that was assigned to him by Florentine law and
custom. With a mystique such as this he makes a suitable *typus*
for the kind of Magus that might now be envisioned.

For at the same time, the Magi were changing in the eyes of
educated Florentines. As Ficino saw them, the Magi were not the
flamboyant kings envisioned during the later Middle Ages, but
"philosopher-rulers" with an understanding of "natural" laws—
not unlike the Wise Men we imagine today.[100] The change in
conception is nicely reflected in the activities of the Compagnia
de' Magi. The confraternity seems gradually to have lost interest
in the sumptuous pageant which attracted the notice of many
observers during the first three decades or so of Medici rule. Its
attention was drawn to two mystical forms of devotion: one
based on penitence, the other on the notion of the spirit's ascent
toward God.[101] The rewards at stake were very high: the salvation of the brothers' souls. In this Pelagian atmosphere the Magi
are invoked again and again in the confraternity's sermons as
examples to be followed and as benevolent guides.[102] They are
no longer exotic and remote, but psychically near—imitable
through an act of worship.

Thus the Medici and the Magi might be brought together. But
if the Medici appear in Botticelli's picture, decorum has still had
its say. The full equation would hold only for Cosimo and Piero,
both of whom were dead when the altarpiece was painted. And
the dead are, conventionally, beyond reproach. The living, Lorenzo and Giuliano, could not, it seems, be recognizable and Magi

[97] *Opera omnia*, I, p. 648: "Multum equidem Platoni nostro debeo, sed
Cosmo non minus debere me fateor. Quam enim virtutum ideam Plato
semel mihi monstraverat, eam quotidie Cosmus agebat. . . ."
[98] By Buser, *Die Beziehungen der Mediceer zu Frankreich*, p. 122.
[99] Brown, "Humanist Portrait," pp. 198f.
[100] On Ficino's interpretation of the Magi, see Chastel, *Art et humanisme*,
pp. 246f.
[101] On the change, see Hatfield, "Compagnia," pp. 119-35.
[102] *Ibid.*, pp. 131f., 134, 157f.

at the same time. But they still might approach the ideal condition of the Three Kings. If represented in Botticelli's picture, they may be the only actual persons there who are shown in festive apparel rather than full-length street dress.[103] Thus the brothers might be raised beyond the realm of the ordinary, but not so far as that of saintliness.

It should now be apparent why, if Botticelli in fact portrayed some of the Medici in his altarpiece, he represented them as types. For that is what they would have to be in his parlance in order to double as Biblical figures. In the Quattrocento one thought of two basic kinds of portrait image. One was our "likeness," which was often described by the term (*vera*) *effigies*. The other was our "idealized portrait," then sometimes called *imago* or occasionally *idea*. The term *effigies*, a record of a person's appearance, implies both actuality and historicity. In his likeness a person is shown as he is or was, the bad and the accidental along with the good and the exemplary. An *effigies* might have magical properties, and it belonged to a lower or manual class of artifacts. But in an *imago* or *idea* a person is shown as he ought to be or have been. The good and the exemplary in him are, through a process of selection or ideation, separated from the bad and the accidental. The *imago* or *idea* had moral properties and, in that it presupposed the exercise of reason, belonged to a higher class of artifacts. Now, taken as wholes the personalities of Cosimo, Piero, Lorenzo, and Giuliano de' Medici could not be held to be "typical" of the Magi—not even by their most ardent admirers. But the qualities they exemplified as "types" might indeed be thought to be Magi-like.

In the frescoes of Benozzo Gozzoli (Figs. 22-24) there appear to be accurate likenesses of members of the Medici. But the presence of these likenesses gives rise to sharp breaks in esthetic continuity within the paintings as a whole. For the effigies of the Medici here are passive in character and frozen in attitude. They are kept well apart from the idealized protagonists, who alone convey most of the action and the moral thrust (such as it

[103] It may be noted here that the hat held by the erect figure behind Caspar is quite similar to that of the old Magus.

is) of the frescoes. The actual and the exemplary are largely separate. If he has depicted the four Medici in his altarpiece for Guasparre dal Lama, Botticelli has here taken a major step in bringing together what Benozzo had kept apart. For here, probably for the first time in Florentine painting, recognizable lay persons would be shown, if somewhat tentatively, in the roles of active, "animated" participants in a Biblical action—both interspersed and interchanged with the agents of the narrative.[104] The idea is in any case more fully developed in the altarpiece by Filippino Lippi for San Donato a Scopeto (Fig. 62), where the several Florentines present at the Epiphany are scarcely different in figuration from the protagonists (at least one of whom probably represents an actual person)[105] and thus enter without break in esthetic continuity into the narrative fabric of the painting. A complete union is afterwards given by Raphael, to whom a synthesis of the actual and the ideal seems to have come without effort, in the numerous portraits he did in the *Stanze* of the Vatican (Fig. 52). What Botticelli may have accomplished in the portraits of his altarpiece need hardly come as a surprise. For his somewhat tentative assimilation of the ideal and the actual in the figures of the four Medici would be in perfect keeping with

---

[104] Meller ("Cappella," pp. 200-22) has claimed that Gian Galeazzo Visconti is portrayed as Theophilus and Coluccio Salutati as his secretary in Masaccio's *St. Peter Raising the Son of Theophilus* in the Brancacci Chapel. I consider both these identifications doubtful. (In the event that they are correct, I believe that Masaccio used these persons only as suitable types for the figures they represent, without further significance.) Meller's identifications as artists of some of the bystanders caught up in the action of Masaccio's *St. Peter Healing with His Shadow* (pp. 287-304) is equally open to doubt, since it rests upon treacherous evidence. The figure of John VIII Paleologus, whom Piero della Francesca represented as Constantine in his frescoes in San Francesco at Arezzo, may well have been intended allegorically. If so, the portrait may be considered an important antecedent to the eventual portraits of members of the Medici as Magi in Botticelli's altarpiece. In any case it is clear that Botticelli would have gone beyond Piero in combining the ideal with the actual, since Paleologus was for most Florentines or others in their dominion a much more remote figure than members of the family which controlled their republic.

[105] The face of the old Magus appears to be a portrait which was modified by the addition of a beard (see above, note 78). The figure of at least one of the bystanders engaged in the action is certainly a portrait. This is the oratorlike man at the right, who was also portrayed by Filippino in the additions he made in Masaccio's *St. Peter Raising the Son of Theophilus* in the Brancacci Chapel. Meller ("Cappella," pp. 189f.) believes him—mistakenly, in my opinion—to be Piero del Pugliese.

the kinds of conflation that occur in the symbolic structure of
the picture. If he indeed has portrayed the Medici in the painting, Botticelli, in involving them in its action, seems to have hit
upon a means for representing the "movements of the soul" of
actual persons in paintings of religious events. Is this not what
Vasari sensed and what led him to praise the portrait he perceived in Botticelli's old Magus as "lifelike" and "natural"?

The figure of Guasparre dal Lama in Botticelli's altarpiece was
identified by Jacques Mesnil just after the turn of this century
(Fig. 53). Mesnil discovered that Guasparre was born around
1411 and therefore reasoned that he must be the old man in the
group of bystanders at the right, just in back of the erect figure
behind Caspar.[106] One would think Mesnil's point sufficient. But
in fact his identification has rarely been sustained.[107] It has already
been observed that the young Magus, among whose followers the
old man is placed, is Guasparre's namesake. One further observation may be made. The old man is the only figure in the painting
who points to himself. A convention which can be found in many
paintings from the last three decades of the Quattrocento, this
gesture is an obvious device for drawing attention to the patron
or some other important person.[108]

[106] Mesnil, "Quelques documents," p. 94.
[107] Mesnil's identification was followed by Bode (*Botticelli*, p. 57).
Unaware of Guasparre's biography, Horne (*Botticelli*, p. 42) suggested
that he might be the dark-haired man looking out from the group of
figures at the left, whom Vasari and Bronzino took for Lorenzo di Giovanni
de' Medici (Figs. 19-21; see above, note 7).
[108] Botticelli used the gesture four times in his *Wedding Feast of Nastagio
degli Onesti* (Fig. 13), where it applies to Antonio Pucci, the patron (or
father of the man for whose marriage the painting was commissioned; he
is the fifth figure from the left at the right-hand table), to Lorenzo de'
Medici (on his identity see above, esp. note 44), and to two other persons
who have not been identified. The gesture is also found in two other
pictures of the Adoration, one by Cosimo Rosselli and the other by Ghirlandaio. In Cosimo Rosselli's painting (Figs. 25, 26) the gesture may have
been used among other things to denote the patron. In Ghirlandaio's (Fig.
61) it may have been used solely for that purpose. Both pictures appear
to have been commissioned by persons connected with the Medici. Cosimo
Rosselli's *Adoration* was probably commissioned by Giovanni Rucellai or
one of the immediate members of his family (see above, note 20). Ghirlandaio's is evidently identical with the tondo of the Adoration that Vasari

Guasparre may here be seen as an imitator of the Magi. For he, too, has made his offering to Christ's "Body." To that act the painting—like Guasparre's chapel an "oblation" itself—bears clear witness. Guasparre's offering of course has an explicitly Eucharistic sense. Lay oblations in kind may have been performed right in front of the picture.[109] And the shoot of laurel growing from the wall over Guasparre's head, as well as the peacock nearby (Fig. 4), both symbols of eternal life, seem clear indications of the benefits which the sacrifice may bring him. In Botticelli's allegory separate moments and places are reconciled through the action of the Eucharist.[110] For by joining into it one is united with Christ's "Body" (which Mary, traditionally a representative of the Church, is proffering not only to the Magi but to their followers as well) and thus with the whole of Christianity. And so Guasparre may plausibly be with his patrons on their visit to Christ.

According to St. Bernard, Guasparre's patrons, the holy Magi, are the "Idea" of those to be saved.[111] Clearly Guasparre counted on their intervention on his behalf. But was his devotion to them only spiritual? In Botticelli's painting the chain of intercessors that leads from Christ to Guasparre is most elaborate. It passes from the old Magus to the central Magus and on to Caspar, Guasparre's namesake. But it does not stop there. For Guasparre is separated from Caspar by the erect figure, with whom he is firmly associated by means of the sprays of laurel growing out of the wall above both their heads (Fig. 4). Are the Medici represented in Botticelli's picture? If so, it seems that Guasparre hoped for as much from his patrons in this life as in the hereafter. With its altarpiece in place, Guasparre may have thought

---

saw in the palace of Giovanni Tornabuoni (Vasari-Milanesi, III, p. 258). Two of the youths who kneel in its foreground appear also to have been portrayed by Ghirlandaio in the Tornabuoni Chapel (Cappella Maggiore) in Santa Maria Novella. If in Ghirlandaio's tondo the pointing, turbaned figure behind the kneeling youths is indeed the patron, he apparently is not Giovanni Tornabuoni himself, but perhaps one of the banker's brothers or nephews.

[109] See above, Chapter II, note 91.

[110] Above, Chapter II, pp. 66f.

[111] *Sermones de tempore*, "In vigilia Nativitatis Domini sermo vi," in Migne, *Patrologia Latina*, CLXXXIII, cols. 112-14. See also Crombach, *Primitiae*, p. 152.

his chapel efficacious indeed. Although it must have cost him dearly, he may well have had cause to think the money well spent.

Botticelli appears also to have represented himself among the followers of the young king. He is probably the red-haired young man looking out at the spectator from the right-hand edge of the picture (Fig. 54).[112] This figure's body is, with its forward thrust, the only one in the painting which illusionistically challenges its imaginary surface. In placement, gaze, and pose the figure conforms to accepted conventions for self-portraits in narrative scenes.[113] The figure likely to be that of Sandro Botticelli is not in line with those of the erect figure behind Caspar and Guasparre dal Lama. Still, the serpentine progression from patron to patron is evident enough. May this be another indication that the young Botticelli was counting on his work for Guasparre to gain him the favor not only of the holy Magi, but also of the powerful family they may here represent?

[112] He was thus identified by Ulmann (*Botticelli*, p. 59). Most subsequent critics have accepted Ulmann's identification. It is possible, but not probable, that Botticelli instead portrayed himself in the dark-haired figure at the left whom Vasari and Bronzino took for Lorenzo di Giovanni de' Medici (Figs. 19-21).

[113] The same type of figure was used for their self-portraits by Benozzo Gozzoli in his frescoes of the Cappella Maggiore of Sant'Agostino at San Gimignano (Fig. 55; Benozzo is the figure at the far right), and by Ghirlandaio in his frescoes in the Sassetti Chapel and again in those in the Cappella Maggiore of Santa Maria Novella (Figs. 56, 57).

IV

The Composition

THERE is good reason to believe that Botticelli meant his Uffizi *Adoration* as a tour de force which might not only gratify Guasparre dal Lama, but also gain himself the attention of the leading patrons of his day.[1] Cast in that mode of nervous elegance which seems to have found great favor with wealthy Italians of the last decades of the Quattrocento, the painting seems perfectly suited to the craving for ornateness and inventiveness that was abroad at the time. Botticelli's contemporaries cannot have overlooked the "rare fancies" and the varied disposition and attitudes in the figures with which Vasari was so taken.[2] Nor can they have remained insensible to the eloquent touches in the setting or the painstaking passages of exact description and fine gilding, many of them now abraded, which the painting displayed. Not that Botticelli has allowed a preoccupation with ornateness for its own sake to lead to that abandon which the more sophisticated of his day might have taken for a lack of understanding of the rules of true art.[3] Botticelli's manipulation of the chief elements in the painting—predominantly straight, slender shapes allowed only exceptionally, and then judiciously, to depart from the true—confers upon it a sense of neatness which belies their considerable number. In its skillful arrangement the picture answers to an urge to orderliness which pervaded not only the artistic notions but indeed the whole genteel culture of Botticelli's day.

[1] See above, Introduction, p. 7; and Chapter III, p. 89.
[2] Above, Introduction, pp. 5f.
[3] On the appreciation of paintings in Botticelli's day, see now Baxandall, *Painting and Experience in Fifteenth Century Italy*.

In the hands of a lesser painter, one imagines, the subject matter of Botticelli's altarpiece would have led to a work of hopeless confusion. Botticelli seems not only to have kept his imagery under control but elegantly to have smoothed over its moral and intellectual equivocations. Still, the complex notions with which Botticelli seems to have been dealing have left their mark upon the painting. For Botticelli has not reconciled them without strain. (Or, conversely, he *has* reconciled them with the kinds of strain of which Vasari approved.) The composition is overbearing and staid in its frontality, without the ease that Botticelli was to achieve in his Mellon *Adoration* of some eight years or so later (Fig. 60). The figures who cluster at either side are curiously brittle and lacking in substance, more "Ideas" of people than flesh and blood. Botticelli's contours are wiry; there is as yet little in the painting of the melodious line which magically plays through both figures and their surroundings, defying gravity as it goes, that Botticelli was to develop in his *Primavera* and go on to perfect as the hallmark of his style. The colors are stringent and rather flat, with little of the richness and integration of hue that one finds in the Mellon *Adoration*. For the most part they are confined to the primaries and purples in the figures, and whites, grays, and browns (some of which may once have been greens) in the setting. In his altarpiece for Guasparre dal Lama, Botticelli, it seems, was concerned more with the world of ideas than with that of pictorial form as such.

But he also seems clearly to have been concerned with the situation of his painting. It is curious that Botticelli, who in most of the works he produced during the early 1470s seems to have been experimenting with the style of Antonio Pollaiuolo, should for the most part have renounced that style in his altarpiece. There is only one figure, that of the young man with the sword at the left, which is clearly of Pollaiuolesque origin. It is an adaptation of the figure at the right of the scene of *Zacharias Leaving the Temple*, of perhaps the mid-1460s, from the series of embroideries done from Pollaiuolo's designs which is now in the Museo dell'Opera del Duomo (Fig. 67). But for the rest, except perhaps for one or two of the more exotic bystanders, Botticelli's *Adoration* seems much crisper in style than anything in Pollaiulo's art. It appears, rather, to reflect an effort on Botticelli's part to come to terms with the great monumental tradition in

Florentine painting. In its firm outlines and volumes it brings to mind some of the grander compositions of Giotto, Masaccio, and Fra Angelico. And the insistent wiriness of Botticelli's contours, sacrificing the quivering spontaneity and atmosphere of Pollaiuolo's style for the sake of solidity, seems rather in the spirit of Andrea del Castagno—even though Botticelli's real exposure to the art of Castagno was to come only with his commission to do the hanged men over the door of the customs house in 1478.

Of his works of the early 1470s, the Uffizi *Adoration* is not the only one in which Botticelli turned from the style of Pollaiuolo. He also did so in the *St. Sebastian*, once in Santa Maria Maggiore and now at Berlin, which was done in January of 1474 (Fig. 68). Here, too, the stark presentation of the saint, with its straight, incisive outlines and clear, columnar volumes, seems to hark back to the monumental tradition. Could it be that in these works Botticelli was deliberately adapting his style to a public mode of religious representation? For the *St. Sebastian*, like the Uffizi *Adoration*, was painted for general view in a church, whereas those works in which a Pollaiuolesque freedom of style is most evident, mostly small in format, seem mainly to have been destined for private places.

Now, the *Adoration* for Guasparre dal Lama, a painting of modest dimensions for an altarpiece, was not designed for an advantageous situation. Visible from any position within the nave of Santa Maria Novella up to the choir screen which cut the present nave into approximate halves, it must often have been almost impossible to see. It had to compete with a brilliant marble frame and an openwork screen which may have hidden it in part to the view of anyone who was not standing close at hand. More serious, it had to contend with light conditions which must have been disastrous. With the main door of the church open, the glare, especially on bright days, must have obscured the painting completely from all but the very closest vantage points. And when the door was closed, the picture must have been all but lost in the gloom of one of the darkest reaches of the great nave. Botticelli seems to have been aware of the difficulties and to have taken measures to counter them. Surely, one of the functions of the painting's regular, rather doctrinaire composition was to enable the little picture to "project" to a considerable distance. And the high saturation of the colors used for a number of the figures, some of which are almost entirely unmodelled, must have served a similar purpose. As one sees it now in the Botticelli Room of the Uffizi, the painting seems strident—and curiously ambivalent —in coloration. But it had to contain some aggressive colors if it was to hold its own in its bright marble frame and to penetrate the gloom of Santa Maria Novella's nave.

The dominant color in the figures of Botticelli's picture is an intense red, which, with slight variations in hue, is more or less evenly distributed among the figures with a strong focus in the central Magus. Botticelli's red is a color that responds most favorably to a soft reddish or yellowish light. In such a light it sheds its shrillness and takes on a warmth that no other color can achieve. Now, this light is of course that produced by candles— the only artificial light by which Botticelli's painting is likely to have been seen before the invention of the electric bulb. Illuminated by candles, the picture cannot have been visible at a great distance. But for persons within the openwork perimeter of Guasparre dal Lama's chapel, it must, with its touches of gold, have provided a rich glow which no visitor to the Uffizi has ever experienced.

The altarpiece for Guasparre dal Lama is the first important Florentine altarpiece of the Epiphany that survives in which the action is centrally placed. The formula in previous compositions called for the Holy Family to be placed at one side, with the Magi and their followers spread across the foreground and into depth upon the other. This formula usually entailed a high point of view in order that the approaching train of the Magi might be clearly visible. Its advantages are obvious. The Magi are seen moving across the spectator's field of vision. Their journey toward Christ is apparent, and their lateral motion may be understood as a sign of their devotion. In nearly all Adorations of the first seven decades of the Quattrocento, the Magi, kings, are shown according to "worldly" convention, the modes of which have clear parallels with those of literary genres such as the romance. Richness, variety, "inventiveness," and even outright preciosity are at a premium. But the Holy Family, in Florence at least, could not decorously be shown in a worldly vein. This difficulty is nicely gotten around in the lateral composition, which permits modulation from the opulence of the Magi to the simple dignity of the Holy Family.

All of these properties are illustrated by Gentile da Fabriano's *Adoration of the Magi* of 1423 (Fig. 10),[4] which appears to have set the trend for most subsequent Adorations for some fifty years. Throughout this period the Albertian rules are simply suspended. With some exceptions, the Florentine Adoration of the early and mid-Quattrocento has a logic of its own, in which movement, detail, naturalism, and the nominal values of fine things all play a role they do not have in monumental representations of most other themes.

It can hardly be a coincidence that the finest examples of the lateral type of Adoration were painted at a time when the Florentine Festa de' Magi was at its height. Florentines knew it as a splendid procession, full of fineness and variety, and a *sacra rappresentazione*, perhaps quite simple, enacted on a platform in front of San Marco.[5] But the Epiphany imagined during these years was not the one that was envisioned by Botticelli and his more sophisticated contemporaries. Doubtless they had some lingering impression of it. But for them the Magi were no longer fabulous representatives of a lost world, whose actions might be imitated, but only in externals. Rather, they were coming to stand for a comprehensible state of mind.[6]

The centralized composition was taken up in the north by Roger van der Weyden in the central panel of his Columba Altarpiece (Fig. 59) perhaps twenty years before Botticelli in the altarpiece for Guasparre dal Lama.[7] Roger probably painted his *Adoration* with the great altarpiece of the town hall of Cologne in mind (Fig. 58). That picture, which Albrecht Dürer mentions in his

[4] On Gentile's painting, see Paatz, *Kirchen*, v, pp. 261f., 308f.
[5] On the Festa de' Magi, see Hatfield, "Compagnia," pp. 108-19.
[6] On this change, see above, Chapter III, p. 95.
[7] On the Columba Altarpiece, see Panofsky, *Early Netherlandish Painting*, pp. 249-51, 286-88; and Arndt, *Rogier van der Weyden, Der Columba-Altar*.

Netherlandish Journal (he had to pay to see it), was painted in the 1440s by Stefan Lochner.[8] Fundamentally iconic, it shows the Virgin and Child with Saints, among whom the Magi, the foremost patrons of the city, appear in posts of special honor. There is but slight reference to the action of the Epiphany. In the *Adoration* of the Columba Altarpiece, probably painted for the mayor of Cologne,[9] Roger evidently wanted to capture the sense of the iconic altarpiece without sacrificing his narrative.

This of course is what Botticelli undertook to accomplish in his altarpiece for Guasparre dal Lama. Like Roger he was evidently familiar with a representation of the Magi before Christ in which narration is completely sacrificed to iconic significance. That picture was probably the altarpiece attributed to Francesco d'Antonio (Fig. 5), although it might have been another painting of the same type which is now lost.[10] But the intricate structure of the altarpiece for Guasparre dal Lama is far removed from the lifeless composition of the earlier picture or anything like it. If Botticelli referred to it for his symbolism, he does not seem to have studied its form. As a painting, Botticelli's altarpiece seems chiefly to depend on Fra Filippo's Cook tondo, Botticelli's own previous experience in depicting the Epiphany, and his inspection of the thematic material with which he had to deal.

In the Cook tondo (Fig. 11) the lateral composition is seri-

[8] On the Altarpiece of the Town Saints, see Stange, *Die deutschen Tafelbilder vor Dürer*, I, p. 42, no. 95.

[9] Arndt, p. 3; Beenken, *Rogier van der Weyden*, p. 84.

[10] See above, Chapter II, note 9. It may be that Botticelli decided to place the action in the center of his picture in order to bring out the importance of the Magi, who seem to have had greater significance for Guasparre dal Lama than for most other persons who commissioned paintings of the Epiphany. (This may also have been true in the case of the altarpiece attributed to Francesco d'Antonio; see above, Chapter II, note 12.) Guasparre's chapel was founded under the title, "The Three Magi on the Day of the Epiphany of Our Lord, Jesus Christ" (above, Chapter I, p. 31). Although its altar seems properly to have been consecrated to the Epiphany of the Lord (*ibid.*), one may imagine that in Guasparre's mind the dedication was to the Magi. If indeed there were any at all, altars consecrated to the Magi as such must have been very few in Florence during the Quattrocento. One may have been in the oratory of the Compagnia de' Magi. Another may have been the Altar of the Magi before the *tramezzo*, now destroyed, of Santa Maria del Carmine, which is mentioned in a *Libro de' Patronati* of that church (ASF, Conventi Soppressi, 113, 13, pp. 7, 37f.) and in the testament of its founder, Giovanni di Lamberto Manetti, drawn up in 1449 (ASF, Notarile Antecosimiano, F 304 [Ser Filippo di Cristofano di Leonardo, 1449-53], fols. 74r-75v).

ously challenged for the first time in Florentine paintings of the Epiphany.[11] The Holy Family is placed somewhat below and to the right of center in the circular field. The shed, normally put at the side, is in the right center. The retinue of the Magi pours down through a gate at the upper left and, as if guided by the picture frame, curls around so that the Magi spread into the lower middle. The old Magus is somewhat nearer the spectator than is the Madonna and Child. Thus the Holy Family is seen in elevation and facing slightly outwards rather than in strict profile. The scene as a whole is dominated by a rock, no doubt the ancestor of the rock behind the Holy Family in the altarpiece for Guasparre dal Lama. As never in compositions of the purely lateral type, the Cook tondo is alive with the movement of shapes and flashes of color. It is a unified metaphor of devotion, without abrupt modulations in style from uninhibited pattern to "rational" simplicity.

The formal organization of the Cook tondo proceeds logically from its circular format. Botticelli was therefore unable to do much with it in his first essay on the Epiphany, the oblong *Adoration* at London (Fig. 12),[12] except borrow some of its motives such as the ruins and a number of the figure types. In this picture the still inexperienced painter had little choice but to take over the lateral arrangement. But he seems to have been reluctant to accept the kinds of stability that it imposes. His figures do not fall into the neat groups that are the rule. On the contrary, Botticelli seems to have let no opportunity for introducing variety go by. One may suppose that he was bent upon generating a sense of excitement like the one he must have felt before the Cook tondo. If so, he has succeeded only in part, because the picture is in many respects out of control.

As if overcompensating for the defects of the oblong picture, Botticelli has turned his tondo at London (Fig. 14), which may have been painted a year or two before the altarpiece for Guasparre dal Lama,[13] into an exercise in orthodoxy. Evidently conscious now of doctrine, Botticelli has applied the rules of perspective in epic dimension. The result is a rigidity of composition

---

[11] On the Cook tondo, see Pittaluga, *Filippo Lippi*, pp. 211-13.

[12] On the oblong panel, see Davies, *Earlier Italian Schools*, pp. 97f.; and Salvini, *Botticelli*, i, pp. 42f.

[13] On the tondo, see Davies, pp. 101f.; and Salvini, i, pp. 44f.

that is otherwise unexampled in his art. In the tondo Botticelli seems to be exploring the hieroglyphic potential of form. Having been given the conventional sign of the circle by the format of the picture, he sets within it the equally conventional sign of the triangle. This somewhat arbitrary solution is "rationalized" by the relentless perspective of the great ruin that looms at the top of the picture. But Botticelli is trapped by the logic of his own conceit. In order to maintain scale, he has had to keep the figures quite small. Although on center, the Madonna and Child have little of the power of the devotional image. One may experience the action as if among the followers of the Magi. But the central action is too distant for one to become fully engrossed in it. In the other figures there is animation, but even their most frenzied actions are too small to compete with the regularity of the composition and thus be perceived as persuasive states of mind.

The subject matter of the altarpiece for Guasparre dal Lama calls for a harmonization of elements which, until the time it was painted, had usually been regarded as antitheses. Botticelli sought to combine narration with doctrine. In the language of pictorial convention this meant movement with stasis, variety with regularity, and consequence of action with frontality. The picture was to deal with an epic "history" and yet be a passive object of worship; it was to be at once an "objective" representation of a bygone occurrence and a "subjective" summons to devotion. For a painter this meant several things. It meant that the picture had to have many figures, but that some of these—especially the Madonna and Child, the "cult" image—had to be given a sense of numinous grandeur. It meant that the action had to be self-contained, but that a means of psychic access had to be provided for the worshipper. Since the picture was to be a "history," it had to convince in terms of "reason" and physical reality. There was no opportunity for escape into pure allegory such as the ones that presented themselves to Botticelli on several other occasions.

Botticelli's altarpiece was painted at a moment in history, for persons of given sophistication and sensibility. He could not have recourse to metaphors based on the properties of gold and other

fine materials such as those which Gentile da Fabriano had used
(even if he did not reject them entirely). But the loss of such
opportunities was, as often, offset by the gain of others. Intellectual changes in Florence had prepared the way for kinds of
"imitation" and "figures" that had not been available to Gentile.
Botticelli might reconcile, as Gentile might not, the ideal with
the actual, the remote with the present, and external reality with
internal experience.

Botticelli has focussed his narrative upon the interplay between
the old Magus and the Holy Family, who confront each other
with the responsiveness of open- and close-quotation marks. The
younger Magi are occupied with concerns of their own, which
however are clearly pertinent to the central action. Most of the
bystanders are watching either of the sets of protagonists. In
response to what they see they stand in attitudes of contempla-
tive respect or lean in active devotion.

Since Mary and the Child are engaged in the narrative, they cannot simultaneously be occupied with the worshipper. In order
to give his Madonna the force of a cult image, Botticelli has
toyed with her scale—but almost imperceptibly. More important,
he has raised her up, upon her "throne," so that she is uncon-
cealed. Thus freed from spatial confinement, and perfectly aligned
with the central Magus, she is pressed forward toward the worshipper by the frontal barrier of the shed, which itself is set
against the upper edge of the picture. One senses Mary, as one
would in iconic altarpieces, as an immanent presence. Botticelli
has taken a low point of view, so that the figures of the central
group, one with the mass of the rock behind them, loom up as
monumental, numinous beings, who bend in response to the
devotion of the old Magus.

The device Botticelli used for locating his narrative in the
esthetic context of doctrine is similar to the one he employed
in his tondo at London. Only here the geometry is far less obtrusive. Nowhere identified with hard or fixed forms, it is subtly
worked into the figures, some of whom are in motion. The basic
triangle, from which the picture derives its stability, culminates
in the enthroned Madonna. Its left side runs through the body
of the old Magus; across the arms of two of the bystanders, one
of whom leans forward, ostensibly to get a better view; and along
the hands and cloak of the man who gestures to the young man
with the sword. Its right side runs along a faint shadow on the

wall and the head and cloak of the onrushing figure behind the young Magus. Only the apex of the triangle, the head of Mary, is accented. But its abstracting force, too, is countered by the placement of Joseph above Mary and to her left. The main system of perspective is focussed not upon Mary, but near the veiled ciborium, which thus receives its due in terms of pictorial doctrine. The circle is worked in, with like subtlety, through the heads of the bystanders nearest the central group and those of the younger Magi. Where the circle might have been broken by the thrusting shape of the old Magus, a shadow line occurs to help it along. One may see it flatly, as a crescent which cradles the Holy Family; or in depth, as an exedra which encloses it.

All of this is grounded in a scheme which ensures an even distribution of shapes over the surface of the picture. For there appears to be more than a hint of an underlying modular structure in the gridlike network that is established by the regular sequence of vertical and horizontal lines in the setting. Even the figures seem to be controlled by the subtle yet pervasive insistence of Botticelli's gridlike scheme.

In doing these things Botticelli was again flirting with rigidity, the peril of which he has countered by a number of means. One is his selection of a second system of perspective for the ruin in the left background. But most important are the emphatic clusters of bystanders that balance the picture on either side, with the power both to convey states of mind and to provide the variety of which Vasari was to make so much in his description of the painting. They are neither too small, as in the London tondo, nor disconnected, as in the oblong panel.

Out of all of this Botticelli has derived the devotional qualities of the altarpiece. The vanishing point of the main system of perspective is near the veiled ciborium. A worshipper standing in front of the altar was thus brought into relation to the ciborium (the subjective present), which in turn was one of his means of spiritual access to the Epiphany (the objective past). Since the ciborium is low in the picture, one is brought into the scene at about the height one's eyes would be if one were kneeling there. Hence the worshipper, embraced by the screen which defined the area of the chapel, might join spiritually into the congregation of the Magi—which has separated to invite him in—and mystically into the whole of Christianity. Three secondary points of access are in the bystanders who look out toward the worshippers, the most assiduous of whom, one imagines, were persons connected with Guasparre dal Lama. One of the outlooking by-standers is of course Guasparre himself, whose gesture also helps to attract attention. He is linked to Christ by an elaborate sequence of advocates, who thus might intercede for these special worshippers as well.

Although its Eucharistic symbolism was rarely taken up again, both the motive of ancient ruins and the centralized composition in the altarpiece for Guasparre dal Lama became standard for subsequent Florentine paintings of the Epiphany. After 1475 no important Florentine picture of the Magi is without them until Andrea del Sarto's fresco of the *Journey of the Magi* of 1513 in the forecourt of the Santissima Annunziata. Two paintings in particular seem to owe a great deal to the example of Botticelli's altarpiece. One is the altarpiece by Filippino Lippi for San Donato a Scopeto (Fig. 62),[14] in which the shed and the disposition of the main figures clearly owe much to Botticelli's. The other is the painting for which Filippino's was made as a substitute, the great unfinished *Adoration*, now in the Uffizi, by Leonardo da Vinci (Fig. 63). That picture, commissioned in March of 1481 by the Canons Regular of San Donato and evidently abandoned by Leonardo late in the same year, is generally regarded as the opening manifesto of the High Renaissance style in painting.[15]

It seems curious that the connection between Botticelli's *Adoration* and that of Leonardo has rarely been noticed.[16] That Leonardo's picture is, broadly speaking, indebted to Botticelli's is beyond doubt.[17] In his *Adoration* for Guasparre dal Lama, Bot-

[14] On the altarpiece for San Donato a Scopeto, see Scharf, *Filippino Lippi*, pp. 49-51.

[15] On the unfinished *Adoration*, see Clark, *Leonardo*, pp. 26-33; and Heydenreich, *Leonardo*, I, pp. 28f. Leonardo's painting has recently been studied by Irene Below (*Leonardo da Vinci und Filippino Lippi*). I find it difficult to accept her contention that it is not identical with the picture commissioned in 1481.

[16] As a rule Leonardo's picture has been examined in the light of Botticelli's only by those writers in search of portrait identities in some of Leonardo's figures (e.g., Müller-Walde, *Leonardo*, pp. 126f.).

[17] The only other altarpiece from which Leonardo might have had much to learn, the *Adoration of the Shepherds* by Hugo van der Goes (Fig. 66), has recently been shown to have reached Florence only in 1483, by which

ticelli had established, probably by 1475, the centralized composition and the motive of prominent ruins, and in 1481 Leonardo
followed suit; there was as yet no other important depiction
of the scene from which he might have derived the idea. But
Leonardo's debt to Botticelli appears to go beyond the simple
adoption of a new pictorial type. For, a number of key compositional elements in Leonardo's picture, some of which were
of central importance in the pictorial revolution upon which
he was now taking the first decisive steps, answer to like elements
in Botticelli's. That the correspondence of these elements to
their counterparts in the Botticelli is not fortuitous, seems proved
by the fact that none of them had been determined upon in
Leonardo's preparatory drawings for his picture. The idea for
them seems to have come to him only when his designs for the
painting were at an advanced stage—when, it seems, he was exposed to some stimulus that caused him to change his mind about
the final form it was to take.

Of the compositional elements in question, surely the most
important is the coordinated triangle and arc which control the
disposition of the figures and which no satisfactory analysis of
Leonardo's picture can fail to mention. It was by means of a triangle and arc that Botticelli had ordered the numerous figures in
his altarpiece for Guasparre dal Lama. Of course in the Leonardo
the idea is differently applied. He has surrounded his central
group from behind in such a manner that the circular mass of
attendant figures opens toward, rather than away from, the
spectator. Thus the arc now surmounts and encloses the triangle,
rather than bisecting it as it had in the Botticelli. The compres-
sive force of Botticelli's shed is no longer needed, and the figures
can be molded into a continuous group similar to, but far more
dense in activity than, the one that Masaccio had used in his
Tribute Money (Fig. 64). Yet even with the reversal a strong
echo remains of Botticelli's composition. For Leonardo's writhing
tangle of figures, aptly likened by Kenneth Clark to the Stream
of Ocean of Ptolemaic geography, performs the same compositional role as the hill that looms up behind Mary and Joseph
in Botticelli's picture. (In fact, Leonardo's group is also set off
by a hill.)

---

year Leonardo had gone to Milan. See B. Hatfield Strens, "L'arrivo del
trittico Portinari a Firenze."

For the terminal points that anchor his composition at either side, Leonardo, like Botticelli, makes use of an elegant youth and of a heavily draped figure. Here, too, the positions have been reversed (rather as if, one is tempted to remark, Leonardo wished to make the point that Botticelli had got things backwards). To be sure, Leonardo's heavily draped "philosopher," based on Masaccio, had already appeared in the preparatory drawings.[18] Still, the "philosopher's" correspondence in the final version to Botticelli's presumed self-portrait, like that of Leonardo's youthful figure to Botticelli's, seems clear enough.[19]

The ruins in Leonardo's picture, entirely of his invention, were already conceived by him in a celebrated preparatory drawing in the Uffizi,[20] in which composition they helped to define the main stage for the action and also served as one of the main supports for the shed. In the final version, for reasons already indicated, Leonardo boldly did away with the shed altogether and moved the ruins into the far distance. There they conform, in both position and perspective, to the ruins in Botticelli's altarpiece.

In the altarpiece for Guasparre dal Lama Botticelli appears to have touched upon the compositional principles of the High Rennaissance.[21] Botticelli was at heart a painter of intellectual

[18] The "philosopher" occurs in the drawing in the Louvre (formerly Galichon Coll.; ill.: Heydenreich, II, fig. 9) which appears to give Leonardo's initial ideas for his figural composition. The grouping here is still quite Quattrocentesque.

[19] Lawrence Lowic has pointed out to me that the relationship of the "philosopher" to the two adjacent figures in the left foreground may reflect the grouping in Giotto's *Ascension of St. John the Evangelist* in the Peruzzi Chapel (Fig. 65).

[20] Ill.: Clark, pl. 12.

[21] He was to approximate them even more closely in the lovely Mellon *Adoration* now in Washington (Fig. 60). This painting was probably done during Botticelli's sojourn in Rome in 1481-82, at which time he also did the three narrative frescoes in the Sistine Chapel (on Botticelli's stay in Rome, see Covi, "Botticelli and Pope Sixtus IV"). The Mellon *Adoration* is generally identified with a painting mentioned by the Anonimo Magliabechiano: "In Roma dipinse anchora. Et fecevj una tavola di Magi che fu la più ——— [sic] opera che maj facessj" (*Il Codice magliabechiano*, p. 105). Thus the Mellon *Adoration* would have been the Anonimo Magliabechiano's favorite Botticelli, as the Uffizi *Adoration* was Vasari's. There are good grounds for believing that the Mellon *Adoration* is indeed the painting to which the Anonimo Magliabechiano was referring. The picture is said to have had a Roman provenance (Salvini, *Botticelli*, I, p. 63; however, it should be noted that the Mellon picture is the only one of Botticelli's extant *Adorations* of which the measurements [71 x 104 cm.] closely approximate those of a painting described in an inventory taken of the

abstractions; much of the time he seems to have been drawn to
find metaphors for casts of mind for which there is no pictorial
equivalent in "rational" experience. But whatever his natural bent,
Botticelli was above all a brilliant analyst of his subject matter.
In the altarpiece for Guasparre dal Lama, Botticelli undertook to
paint a subject which demanded the conflation of several
thoughts. He produced a tour de force of pictorial integration,
establishing harmony through a delicate system of interlocking
structures. Thus Botticelli chanced tentatively to capture a state
of mind in which antithesis is powerless before the intellect. For
reasons for which, it seems clear, he was not entirely responsible,
he achieved a picture that, along with some of the frescoes of
Masaccio, seems to have been the point of departure for Leonardo's first major invention in painting. But the formal integration that Botticelli achieved in the altarpiece remained for him
a means of illustrating interwoven themes and did not become a
guiding esthetic principle in itself. In his altarpiece for Guasparre
dal Lama, Botticelli produced what may be termed a marvel of
pictorial conflation, for which he justly won the approval of
Giorgio Vasari. But the synthesis was Leonardo's.

Medici possessions in the Palazzo del Casino in 1587: "Uno quadro in
tavola con una Natività di Nostro Signore con magi, disson di mano
del Botticelli, alto braccia 1¼, largo braccia 1¾ incirca [about 73 x 102
cm.], con ornamento di legno intagliato e dorato" [ASF, Guardaroba
Medicea, 136, fol. 154r]). The pair of oaks growing just to the right of the
main building may well be an allusion to the arms of the Della Rovere
(Salvini, 1, p. 63). It may also be pointed out that the man seen in profile
in the group of adorants at the right appears to be identical with one of
the persons portrayed in Botticelli's fresco of *The Temptation and the Old
Testament Sacrifice* in the Sistine Chapel (ill.: Salvini, 1, pl. 97), who
probably is either Girolamo Riario, the nephew of Sixtus IV, or one of the
Della Rovere (on his identity, see Salvini, 1, p. 60). Stylistically the painting is clearly a more advanced work than the Uffizi *Adoration*. This seems
evident especially in the greater range of coloration and in the greater ease
of figural integration in the clusters of bystanders at either side. Two
interesting motives also seem to indicate that the Mellon *Adoration* is the
later of the two paintings. One is the tumultuous horses at the right, which
have reminded several critics of those in the unfinished painting by Leonardo. The other is the curious acanthus leaves at the corners of the
capitals of the main building, bending over the flutings below, which
take the place of the volutes that Botticelli used in the Uffizi *Adoration*.
This quite unusual feature is also found in the treatise of Francesco di
Giorgio Martini (*Trattati di architettura, ingegneria e arte militare*, ed.
C. Maltese, Milan, 1967, 1, fol. 15v, pl. 26). I owe this observation to
Lawrence Lowic.

Appendices

1. May 29, 1469. First testament of Guasparre dal Lama (ASF, Notarile Antecosimiano, A 313m [Ser Giovanni Allegri], no. 96, fols. 229r-230v):

Jn Dei nomine amen. Anno dominice jncarnationis millesimo quatuorcentesimo sexagesimo nono, jndictione secunda, die vero vigesimo nono mensis May. Actum Florentie jn conventu sancte Marie Novelle, ordinis Predicatorum. Presentibus testibus ad jnfrascripta vocatis et proprio hore jnfrascriptis [*sic*] testatoris [*sic*] vocatis, habitis et rogatis: magistro Stefano Beni[n]case, priore dicti conventus, magistro Dominico Johannis, magistro Dominico Bartolomej et magistro Silvestro Francisco Filippi, magistro Johanne Carulj, magistro Jacobo Petrj, omnibus sacre theologie professoribus, et fratre Damiano Bartulj, dicti ordinis et conventus sancte Marie Novelle fratribus professis.

Cum nil cert[i]us morte et nil jncertius hora eius, hinc est quod:

Guaspar quondam Zenobij de Lama, presoneta [*sic*] artis Cambij, populj sancti Paulj de Florentia, sanus per Dej gratiam mente, sensu, visu, auditu et jntellectu, totoque corpore, volens per presens suum nuncupativum testamentum, quod dicitur sine scriptis, de suis bonis suam ultimam disponere voluntatem, et [*sic*] suum ultimum testamentum disposuit, fecit et ordinavit jn hunc modum et formam, videlicet:

Jn primis quidem animam suam, cum de hac vita migrari contingerit, humiliter et devote recomendavit omnipotenti Deo, eiusque matri verginis [*sic*] gloriose, totique celestis [*sic*] curie triunphantis [*sic*]. Corpus vero suum sepellirj voluit jn ecclesia sancte Marie Novelle jn capella jnfrascripta et de qua infra fit mentio, cum sumptis et expensis de quibus jnfrascriptis eius executoribus videbitur et placebit.

Jtem reliquit operj sancte Marie del Fiore, et nove sacrestie dicte ecclesie, et constructionj et conservationj murorum civitatis Florentie, et cuilibet dictorum locorum, solidos viginti, videlicet jn totum libras tres.

J[tem] voluit, si et jn quantum et jn casu quo dictus testator decederet sine filijs legitimis et naturalis [*sic*], disposuit, voluit et ordinavit quod jndumenta et pannos [*sic*] et vestes ad dorsum dicti testatoris, et cintolas argenteas [*sic*], anulos [*sic*], chuchiaros [*sic*] et forrghettj de argento et perle et similia per infrascriptos eius executores jncontinentj secuta morte dicti testatoris vendantur et distriantur. Et de pretio et retractu nubantur septtem puellas [*sic*], non excedendo summam librarum septuaginta pro qualibet earum. Residuum vero dicti pretij datur et consignetur, et darj et consignarj voluit, fratribus, capitulo et conventui sancte Marie Novelle de Florentia, amore Dej, cum honere celebrandi missas pro anima dicti testatoris, videlicet tantum quantum amore Dej capitur solidorum quinque pro quolibet sacerdotj qui dictas missas celebrabit.

Jn casu quo ut supra sine filij[s] decesserit, reliquit et legavit domine Cose, eius uxori, podere cum molendino et gualchiera et aliis suis hedifitiis positum jn populo sancte Lucie a Collina, vallis Marine, loco dicto "al Palagio," infra eius loca [*sic*], vocabula, et confines, cum omnibus et singulis petijs terrarum et bonis dicto poderj pertinentibus et expectantibus, et cum omnibus et singulis masseritijs jbidem existentibus, et cum omnibus et singulis besti[i]s bovinis et pecudinis et caprinis et presta laboratoribus; et ultra predicta florenos auri centum, conputatis jn dicto legato florenis aurj ducentis quos pro eius dotibus dixit habuisse et recepisse.

Jtem ultra predicta voluit quod dicta domina Cosa, eius uxor predicta, tempore mortis dicti testatoris jnduatur vestimentis lugubribus secundum morem et consuedudinationem [*sic*] viduarum.

Jtem jn casu quo ut supra sine fili[i]s decesserit, et jn casu quo dicta domina Cosa, eius uxor predicta, velit viduam stare et vitam vidualem et honestam (?) servare, tunc et eo casu eidem domine reliquit et legavit toto tempore sue vite usum et habitationem domus dicti testatoris posite jn via cuj dicitur "la via della Schala" jn populo sancti Paulj de Florentia, cum omnibus et singulis masseritijs, supelectibus et bonis jn ea existentibus, exceptis illis de quibus supra dicitur quod vendi et distrii debeant pro puellis nubendit [*sic*]. Post vero mortem dicte domine Cose, et seu jn casu quo se nubere voluerit, voluit, disposuit, et ordinavit dictus testator quod omnes masseritie dicti testatoris que tunc tempore jn dicta domo reperientur per jnfrascriptos eius executores presentis testamenti vendantur et distrantur, et de ipsorum pretio peraficatur [*sic*] domus predicta, videlicet jn sala superiorj de camino, aquario et amattonito, cum pancis et cum arco et cum palco superiorj, super quo ad usum quoquine fiat caminus, aquarius, et cum stia murata. De residuo vero pretij dictarum masseritiatum [*sic*] emantur [*sic*] et emj voluit unum lectum fulcitum cum sacone, materasso, caltrice, coltrone et panno vermilio, et duobus paribus linteaminum, jn hospitalj sancti Paulj de Florentia pro remedio anime jpsius testatoris. Residu[u]m vero erogari voluit pro nubendo puellas egenas, non excedendo pro qualibet earum summam librarum septuaginta.

Jtem post mortem dicti testatoris et dicte domine Cose, eius uxoris, et seu postquam dicta domina Cosa se nupsserit et ad secunda vota transiverit, jn casu predicto ex nunc prout ex tunc, et ex tunc prout ex nunc, ex titulo et causa donationis post mortem dedit, donavit, tradidit et concessit capelle que per dictum testatorem construitur jn ecclesia sancte Marie Novelle sub titulo trium Magorum jn die Ephyfanie Dominj nostrj Yhesu Christi dictam domum habitationis dicti testatoris positam in via della Casa [*sic*] jn populo sancti Paulj pro dote et nomine dotis dicte capelle. Et voluit, disposuit et ordinavit dictus testator quod domus predicta nullatenus jn perpetuum vendi, di[s]triy nec alienarj seu ad lo[n]gum tempore [*sic*] locarj modo aliquo possit vel valeat, nisi de quinquennio jn quinquenio, sed perpetuo stare et esse voluit pro dote dicte capelle. De quorum [*sic*] jntroytibus et pensione et usufructu voluit dicta capella [*sic*] per fratres, capitulum et conventum sancte Marie Novelle offitiarj et celebrarj qualibet edemoda(?) jn perpetuo unam missam pro anima dicti dicti [*sic*] testatoris. Jn die vero festivitatis dicte capelle celeb[r]etur jn dicta capella: primo, missa plana; secundo, missa canendo; dejnde tertia, alia missa plana. Et hoc si et jn quantum et postquam causas quod dicta domus ad dictam capellam ut supra devenerit. Et si et in quantum et jn casu quo alienaretur vel venderetur seu ad lon[gu]m tempus locaretur, tunc et in eo casu domus predicta [*sic*] reliquit et legavit hospitalj sancti Paulj de Florentia, cum honere dandi et solvendi quolibet anno dictis fratribus, capitulo et conventui sancte Marie Novelle libras quinquaginta pro offitiando capellam predictam ut supra. Et si et jn quantum et jn casu qau [*sic*] quo dictum hospitale sancti Paulj ut supra dictam domum vendiderint vel alienaverint seu ad longum tempus locaverint [*sic*], tunc et eo casu domum predictam hospitalj sancte Marie Nove cum dicto honere solvendi dictas libras quinquaginta reliquit et legavit. Et si et jn quantum et jn casu quo dictum hospitale sancte Marie Nove ut supra dictam domum vendiderit vel alienaverit seu ad longum tempus locaverit, tunc et eo casu domum predictam Camere Apostolice cum dicto honere solvendi dictas libras quinquaginta ut supra reliquit et legavit.

Jtem si et jn quantum et jn casu quo dictus Guaspar, testator predictus, filios legitimos et naturales habuerit, tunc et eo casu liceat et licitum sit dicto testatorj et dictis eius filiis emere tot bona jnmobilia ad declarationem prioris, fratrum, capituli et conventus sancte Marie Novelle predictorum, pro tempore existentium, que sint redditus anno quolibet librarum quinquaginta. Que bona emantur sub nomine dicte capelle; que sint et sunt perpetuo pro ipsius capelle dote, et quos [*sic*] fructus et redditus sint perpetuo pro offitiando dictam capellam; que nullatenus modo aliquo vendi vel alienarj possi[n]t, prout supra dicitur de domo. Et quod domus ipsa, facta dicta emptione, lib[e]ra dicto Guasparre seu dictis eius filiis remaneat.

Jtem reliquit et legavit Francischo Nicholai Chochi florenos auri centum si et jn quantum et jn casu quo dictus testator ut supra sine filijs decesserit, si dictus Franciscus [*sic*] tempore mortis dicti testatoris vivere contingerit, sive autem filiis maschulis, legitimis et naturalibus dicti Franciscj si eos vivere contingerit tempore mortis dicti testatoris.

Suos autem et huius presentis testamenti et ultime voluntatis executores reliquit, fecit et esse voluit:

> Johannem Laurentij Bencj,
> Bernardum Stoldi Raynerij et
> Pierum Laurentij Capellj,

cives honorabiles Florentinos, et quoscunque duos ex eis in concordia, existente alio enim absente, mortuo vel remoto seu aliqualiter jnpedito, dans et concedens dictus testator dictis eius executoribus, et quibuscunque duobus ex eis jn concordia, existente plenum, liberum, generale et speciale mandatum, [*sic*] etc.

Jn omnibus autem aliis suis bonis mobilibus et jnmobilibus, juribus, nominibus et actionibus presentibus et futuris, sibi universales heredes jnstituit, fecit et esse voluit omnes et singulos eius filios maschulos legitimos et naturales nascicutos [*sic*] ex se et ex quacunque eius uxore legitima, casu quo extarent tempore mortis dicti testatoris. Si vero non extarent maschulj, tunc et eo casu suos heredes ut supra jnstituit eiusdem testatoris filias feminas legitimas et naturales nascituras ex se et ex quacunque eius uxore legitime [*sic*], casu quo extarent tempore mortis dicti testatoris. Casu vero quo non extarent filie femine, tunc et eo casu suam universalem heredem jnstituit, fecit et esse voluit dominam Cosam, eius uxorem legitimam et filiam olim Batiste Leonardi de Empulo, civis Florentini [casu quo vixerit, salvis semper supradictis conditionibus, de quibus supra fit mentio, quibus semper adjnplerj voluit prout jn eis continetur]. Si vero dicta domina Cosa jn humanis non extaret, tunc et eo casu suam universalem heredem jnstituit, fecit et esse voluit dictam capellam sanctorum trium Magorum, de qua supra fit mentio.

2. January 31, 1475/76. Guasparre dal Lama is tried and condemned for fraud by the consuls of the Arte del Cambio (ASF,
Arte del Cambio, 19, *ad datum*):

Jtem consules omnes predictj, attendentes ad quandam scriptam
privatam manu Stefanj Vermiglj Masj fornaciarij et subscriptam
manu jnfrascriptj Ghuasparjs, factam sub die prima Septembris 1450,
continentem jn se, jn effectu, qualiter dictus Stefanus dicit se esse
debitorem dictj Ghuasparjs de libris tricentis soldorum parvorum,
rationibus et causis jn dicta scripta contentis et expressis, anullantes jn
dicta scripta quecunque alia negocia que olim quomodocunque jnter
se egissent, prout predicta latius constant jn dicta scripta privata de
qua supra; et actendentes quod de mense Novembris proxime pre-
terito presentis annj, coram consulibus dicte artjs, dictus Stefanus
suam petitionem jn scriptis porrexit contra dictum Ghuasparem,
petens jn ea ab eo libras trigintatres soldorum parvorum, rationibus
et causis jn dicta petitione expressis; a qua petitione et contentibus jn
ea volens se defendere, dictus Ghuaspar comparuit coram dictis
consulibus et verbo negavit contenta dicte petitionis vera esse, et ad
justificationem jurium suorum, jpsius Ghuasparis; et ut clare constant
jpsis consulibus, negatum [*sic*] per jpsum Ghuasparem vera esse, et
non fore nec esse debitorem dictj Stefanj de et pro quantitate petita,
produxit dictam scriptam et cautionem privatam de qua supra, jn qua
ipse Ghuaspar machulaverat annum jn ea descriptum, videlicet annum 1450, et de figura denominata materno sermone zero apposita
jn principio dicte scripte, fecit aliam figuram jmporta[n]tem numerum
octonarium, adeo quod, cum jm primjs jmportabat annum 1450, post
dictam corruptionem et machulam jmportabat annum 1458. Et hoc
jdeo dixit et confessus fuit dictus Ghuaspar fecisse, machulasse et
alterasse dictum annum quinquagenarium, quia ab dicto anno quinqua-
genario citra jpse Ghuaspar contraxerat dictum debitum librarum
trigintatrium contentum jn dicta petitione dictj Stefanj cum jpso
Stefano, et ante annum 1458, et ut appareret ad jpsum debitum non
teneri propter finem factam jn dicta scripta sub jllis verbis que apposita sunt jn ipsa scripta, videlicet: "Anullando ognj altre nostre
faccende che per lo adrieto o qualunche modo havessimo havuto a
fare jnsieme," etc.; et ut predicta magis verifichare possit et jpsis
consulibus persuadere, produxit etiam quendam librum suum foliorum
communium, cum coverta de chorio viride, choriggia et fibbia, jn
quo libro, carta 11, falsificavit annum et corrasit et machulavit ut
quedam memoria facta sive *richordo* jn dicto libro, carta 11, appareret
recte a debito et congruo tempore descripta esse; quam memoriam

sive *richordo* fecit jpse Ghuaspar ut melius verificaretur falsitatem et corruptelam et maculam per eum factam jn dicta scripta, de qua supra, de dicto anno 1450, falsificato et permutato per eum jn annum 1458; et sic aperte et sponte coram dictis consulibus fassus e[s]t crimen suum et falsitatem seu falsitates sic per eum conmissas jn dicta scripta et libro de quibus supra, rationibus et causis predictis, et ut prejudicaret juribus creditj dictj Stefanj contratos et petitos [*sic*] jn dicta petitione, et ut ad jllud debitum pronuntiarj non posset eum tenerj; et hec omnia conmisit et falsificavit et maculavit malo animo et preter jus et justitiam et bonos mores et jn dampnum et dedecus dictj Stefanj creditorj[s]. Idcirco consules predictj, cognitjs et jntellectis predictis et nonnullis alijs ad predicta facientibus, necnon etiam qualiter jpse Ghuaspar, se defendendum a dicta petitione et contentibus in ea coram consulibus fuit homo mendax, ne de predictis gloriarj possit, et ut sit ceteris exemplo, volentes tamen benigne et humaniter procedere, et ne jn totum justitia pereat, deliberaverunt, et deliberando condempnaverunt dictum:

Ghuasparem Zenobij de Lamole, sensalem chambiorum jn civitate Florentie, jn florenos nonaginta largos, dandos et solvendos camerario dicte artis pro dicta arte, recipienti pro jllis, erogandos et distribuendos ubj et quando et quomodo per dictos consules provisum et deliberatum fuerit, per totum mensem Apriljs proxime futuri annj 1476, jn una vice vel pluribus, cum salvo, etc., quod si dictus Ghuaspar de dicta summa florenorum nonaginta largorum dederit et jntegre persolverit dicto camerario dicte artis per totum mensem Februarij proxime futurj presentis annj florenos quadragintaquinque largos, sit liber et absolutus a dicta maiorj summa, etc., videlicet florenis xxxxv largis.

Jtem consules predictj, ut narratur jn condempnatione dictj Ghuasparjs, de qua supra, [ut] omnibus constare possint, et ne dictus Ghuaspar librum et scriptam de quibus supra jn dicta condempnatione celare possit et negare narrata ut supra vera non esse; jdcirco, servatis servandis, etc., deliberaverunt quod liber dictj Ghuasparis, de quo supra, cum dicta scripta continuo et perpetuo sint jn dicta arte et penes me notarium dicte artis et successores meos, ne quod de dicta arte extrahi possint, nisj precedentj deliberatione consulum dicte artis una congregatorum cum hominibus *del consiglio* artis predicte, obtinendum partitum per vigintj fabas nigras inter omnes, etc. Declarantes tamen quod non obstantibus predictis, liceat dicto Ghuasparj dictum librum producere in quocunque loco et in quacunque curia, casu quo eo utj et producj contingerit pro suis juribus consequendis, ita tamen quod portetur tempore dicte productionis faciende per unum ex famuljs dicte artis, et per eundem famulum reportetur in dictam artem et dicto notario consignetur. Ac etiam liceat dicto

Ghuasparj, quotienscunque voluerit, copiam et exemplar et partitas et computa summere pro suo libito [et] voluntate dummodo de jpsa arte non extrahatur ut supra, etc.

3. March 17, 1477/78. Second testament of Guasparre dal Lama (ASF, Notarile Antecosimiano, P 339 [Ser Piero di Antonio da Campi], no. 86, fols. 224r-225r):

[*In margin*: Revocatum per aliud testamentum, carta 249.]

Jn Dei nomine amen. Anno Dominj ab eius salutifera incarnatione millesimo quadringentesimo septuagesimo septimo, indictione xjª et die xvjjª mensis Martij. Actum in civitate Florentie in populo sancti Marci et in sacrestia dicte ecclesie, presentibus testibus ad infra- scripta omnia et singula vocatis et habitis et ab infrascripto testatore proprio hore rogatis, videlicet: fratre Zenobio Mattie de Florentia, fratre Laurentio Nicholaj de Uzano, fratre Bernaba Simonis de Chanalj, fratre Vincenzio Mattei de Canozio de Gaeta, fratre Cris- tofano Petrj de Mucello, fratre Dominico Paulj de Florentia et fratre Apolinario Jacobj de Butrio, omnibus fratribus in dicta ecclesia, ordinis sancti Dominici, et fratre Ambrosio Jacobj de Mediolano, omnibus fratribus sancti Dominici in dicta ecclesia sancti Marci. [*In footnote*: Jtem amore Dei reliquit, etc., cuilibet dictorum fratrum testium libram unam pro quolibet.]

Quoniam nichil est certius morte et nil incertius eius hora, hinc est quod:

Providus vir Ghuaspar olim Zenobij de Lama, civis Florentinus, populj sancti Paulj de Florentia, sanus Dei gratia mente, sensu, visu, intellectu et corpore, nolens intestatus decedere, et [volens] super dispositione suorum bonorum, rerum et jurium per presens nuncu- pativum testamentum, quod dicitur sine scriptis, disponere, suum nuncupativum condidit testamentum in hunc modum et formam, videlicet:

Jn primis namque animam suam omnipotentj Deo eiusque gloriose matrj, Virginj Marie, et totj celestialj curie paradisj humiliter et devote reconmendavit. Sepulturam autem suj corporis, quando eum de hac vita migrarj contingerit, elegit et esse voluit in ecclesia sancte Marie Novelle de Florentia et in sepulcro eius chappelle de Magis, in quo sepellirj voluit ipsum testatorem et dominam Chosam, eius uxorem legitimam, et quoscunque eiusdem testatoris filios legitimos et naturales, si quos haberet, ipsis volentibus, et non alios quoquo modo.

Jtem reliquit et legavit opere sancte Marie del Fiore de Florentia, et nove sacrestie eiusdem, ac etiam opere et constructioni murorum civitatis Florentie in totum libras duas soldorum parvorum.

Jtem amore Dei et pro remedio anime dictj testatoris, reliquit et legavit septem pauperibus puellis egenis et honestis, in hoc honerans conscientiam [infrascripte sue heredis], libras quinquaginta soldorum parvorum pro qualibet, dandas per infrascriptam eius heredem infra unum annum saltim a die mortis dictj testatoris pro dotibus ipsarum, singula singulis congrue referendo, ipsarum viris et maritis; et illud plus ultra dictas libras quinquaginta, quod et prout eidem domine videbitur, dummodo dictj virj dictarum puellarum dictam quantitatem confiteantur in dotem et seu augumentum vel residuum dotis ipsarum, cum fideiussore saltim uno ydoneo, et promictant dictas dotes reddere et consignare in omnj casu, etc., dictarum dotum reddendarum et seu consignandarum consunto matrimonio, vel solutionem et donationem propter nuptias faciant in forma de jure valida, modis et formis in similibus resiquitis [sic], et de quibus et prout videbitur dicte domine Chose eius uxorj, heredi infrascripte, in hoc etiam honerans conscientiam dicte domine.

Jtem ultra predicta, amore Dei et pro remedio anime dictj testatoris, reliquit et legavit Ginevre, filie Dominici Matj de Legrj, vallis Marine, libras vigintj soldorum parvorum, dandas eidem et seu eius viro et marito tunc temporis, in partem et seu augumentum et subsidium dotis ipsius Ginevre, infra dictum tempus unius annj futurj inmediate post mortem dictj testatoris per infrascriptam eius heredem.

Jtem amore Dei et pro remedio anime sue, reliquit et legavit hospitalj sancte Marie Nove de Florentia et hospitalj sancti Paulj de Florentia, videlicet cuilibet dictorum hospitalium, libras vigintj quinque soldorum parvorum pro quolibet, dandas dictis ospitalibus et seu camerario vel ospitalario eorundiem [sic] infra unum annum proxime futurum a die mortis dictj testatoris.

Jtem pro exhoneratione conscientie sue reliquit et legavit Taddeo . . . . [sic] de Ugolinis, scribano et seu custodj librorum Montis Communis Florentie, libras vigintj soldorum parvorum, dandas eidem Taddeo infra unum annum proxime futurum a die mortis dictj testatoris.

Jtem amore Dei et pro remedio anime sue, reliquit et legavit fratribus, capitulo et convenctuj sancte Marie Novelle de Florentia, anno quolibet in perpe[t]uum a die mortis dictj testatoris, florenum aurj largum pro faciendo anno quolibet a die mortis dictj testatoris, qualibet septima die Januarij, unum annuale cum presbiteris et cera et offitio mortuorum, orando Deum pro anima testatoris predictj, et eo modo et forma prout dictis fratribus, capitulo et convenctuj videbitur. Et ultra predicta reliquit et legavit eisdem fratribus, capitulo et con-

venctui anno quolibet, de mense Maij, post mortem ipsius tes[t]a[to]-
ris, in perpetuum, pro retinendo lampadem [*sic*] accensam ad altare
de Magis, ipsius testatoris, situm in dicta ecclesia, mediam lagenam
olei.

Jtem amore Dei et pro remedio anime sue, reliquit et legavit
fratribus, capitulo et convenctuj sancte Marie Novelle de Florentia,
inmediate sequuta morte dictj testatoris, libras duas soldorum parvorum, et sic successive anno quolibet usque in tres vices et tres an-
nos, libras duas soldorum parvorum pro dicendo et seu dici faciendo
ad dictum altare dictj testatoris missas sancti Greghorij anno quolibet
dictorum trium annorum. Et similiter, pro una vice tamen, reliquit
et legavit fratribus, capitulo et conventuj sancti Marci de Florentia,
libras duas soldorum parvorum, dandas eisdem inmediate sequuta
morte dicti testatoris, pro dicendo et seu dici et celebrarj faciendo in
dicta ecclesia missas sancti Gregorjj pro anima dictj testatoris.

Jn omnibus autem alijs suis bonis mobilibus et inmobilibus, juribus, nominibus et actionibus presentibus et futuris, sibj heredem
universalem instituit, fecit et esse voluit:

Dominam Chosam, uxorem dilectam dictj testatoris et filiam olim
Baptiste Leonardj de Empoli.

Exequutores autem huius testamentj, etc., fecit, reliquit et esse
voluit:

> Johannem Laurentij de Bencijs,
> Bernardum olim Stoldj de Rainerijs et
> Pierum Laurentij de Chappellis,

cives Florentinos, et quoscunque duos ex eis in concordia.

4. August 18, 1480. Guasparre dal Lama acknowledges the receipt
of the dowry of his bride, Angelica di Leonardo Malefici (ASF,
Corporazioni Religiose Soppresse [Conventi Soppressi], 102
[Santa Maria Novella], 106, no. 43; copy made on 18 February
1520/21 from the acts of Ser Nastagio di Ser Amerigo Vespucci):

Guaspar Zenobij de Lama de Florentia, omnj meliorj modo quo
potuit, etc., fuit confessus, etc., habuisse, etc., jn dotem domine
Angelice, eius uxoris et filie Leonardj Luce de Maleficijs de Florentia,
florenos trecentos aurj de sigillo hoc modo, videlicet: florenos du-
centos vigintj et solidos tres ad aurum de sigillo jn pecunia numerata,
et pro ea a Juliano et Antonio de Gondis de Florentia, penes quos
ipsa domina erat creditrix de dictis florenis ccxx solidis iij auri de

sigillo, prout dixerunt patere ad quaternum *dj cassa* ipsorum Julianj et Antonij signato "T" ad 202; residuum vero a dicta domina Angelica jn bonis mobilibus comunj concordia extimatis. Et propterea fecit donationem propter nuptias dicte domine de libris quinquaginta, prout per ordinamenta disponitur. Quas dotes et donationem dictus Guaspar promisit, etc., dicte domine Angelice, licet absenti, etc., et mihi, Anastasio, etc., presenti, etc., reddere, solvere et restituere Florentie, Rome, etc., cum pacto, etc., quod liceat aprehendere tenutam, etc., fructus, etc., non computandos jn sortem, etc. Que omnia, etc., promisit, etc., observare, etc., sub pena florenorum quingentorum largorum, etc. . . .

5. April 21, 1481. Third testament of Guasparre dal Lama (ASF, Notarile Antecosimiano, P 339 [Ser Piero di Antonio da Campi], no. 97, fol. 249r-v):

[*In margin*: Publice restitutum ut hic.
         Data copia ut hic sine loco et testibus Georgio marito
         filie dictj Ghuasparis die 5 Aprilis 1499.]

Jn Dei nomine amen. Anno Dominj ab eius salutifera incarnatione MCCCCLXXXJ, indictione xiiij, et die xxj mensis Aprilis. Actum in civitate Florentie in populo sanctj Paulj de Florentia, presentibus testibus ad infrascripta omnia et singula vocatis et habitis et ab infrascripto testatore proprio hore rogatis, videlicet: Maso Gerij Antonij textore drapporum, Francisco Jacobj Blasij *pannaiuolo* populj sancte Lucie Omnium Sanctorum extra portam Pratj, Antonio Dominici Michaelis textore drapporum populj sancte Lucie predicte intra menia, ser Jacobo Marianj Antonij clerico in ecclesia sancti Paulj, Francisco Antonij Pierj filatoiario populj sanctj Laurentij de Florentia, et Buono Marci del Buono *legnaiuolo* populj sancte Lucie predicte, et Gino Benozj Ginj *legnaiuolo* populj sancti Paulj predictj.

Quoniam nichil est certius morte et nichil incertius eius hora, hinc est quod:

Ghuaspar olim Zenobij de Lama, civis Florentinus, sanus Dei gratia mente, sensu, visu et intellectu, licet corpore languens, nolens intestatus decedere, suum sine scriptis [nuncupativum] condidit testamentum in hunc modum et formam, videlicet:

Jn primis namque animam suam omnipotentj Deo eiusque gloriose matrj, Virginj Marie, [et totj celestj curie paradisj] humiliter et devote reconmendavit. Sepulturam autem suj corporis, quando eum de hac vita migrarj contingerit, elegit et esse voluit in ecclesia sancte Marie Novelle de Florentia ad eius chappellam.

Jtem reliquit et legavit opere sancte Marie del Fiore [de Florentia], et nove sacrestie eiusdem, ac etiam opere et constructioni murorum civitatis Florentie in totum libras tres soldorum parvorum.

Jtem reliquit, voluit, jussit et mandavit quod per infrascriptos eius heredes in perpetuum anno quolibet fiat in ecclesia sancte Marie Novelle de Florentia ad chappellam dictj testatoris unum annuale pro anima dictj testatoris cum cera, missa et presbiteris et aliis requisitis, in quo expendant saltim florenum unum aurj et de auro largum.

Jtem reliquit et legavit amore Dei Ginevre filie Bechj Machj de Legrj libras vigintj soldorum parvorum statim sequuta eius morte.

Jtem reliquit domine [Angelice, eius uxorj dilecte et filie olim Leonardj Luce Malefici,] reditum et expensas victus et vestitus, ipsa vidua stante, una cum infrascriptis eius filiis, et dotes suas non repetente.

Jn omnibus autem alijs suis bonis mobilibus et inmobilibus, juribus, nominibus et actionibus presentibus et futuris, sibj heredem universalem instituit omnem eius filium tam masculum quam feminam, unum et seu plures, nascituros ex eo et domina Angelicha, eius uxore [predicta] et filia olim [dictj] Leonardj Luce Malefici, [equis portionibus] ipsis ad lucem pervenientes et ipsis ad lucem non pervenientes vel pervenientes [sic], et quandocunque decendentibus [sic] sine filiis descendentibus masculis legitimis et naturalibus, sibj heredem instituit et seu substituit dictam dominam Angelicham [eius uxorem predictam]. Et hanc dixit et asseruit dictus testator fuisse suam ultimam voluntatem, quam valere voluit jure testamentj. Et si jure testamentj non valeret, valeat et valere voluit jure codicillorum. Et si jure codicillorum non valeret, valeat et valere voluit jure donationis causa mortis vel alterius cuiuscunque ultime voluntatis, prout melius valere poterit et tenere; capsans, jrritans et anullans omne aliud testamentum et ultimam voluntatem usque in presentem diem per eum facta manu mei, notarij infrascriptj, et cuiuscunque alterius notarij; et quovis modo, non obstante quod in eo, ea vel eis essent apposita aliqua verba derogatoria, penalia vel precisa; etiam si talia forent, de quibus in presentj testamento et clausula revocatoria expressa mentio fierj deberet, de quibus dixit se ad presens non recordarj et omnino penituisse et penitere; et voluit presens testamentum omnibus alijs ipsius testatoris testamentis et ultimis voluntatibus prevalere, et nullo modo vel per aliquam revocationem tacitam vel expressam, generalem vel spetialem infringi, revocarj, capsarj aut aliquo modo irritarj [sed totiens confirmarj et de novo fierj quotiens apparerent modo aliquo irritatum vel viribus vacuatum], nisi in ea [revocatione] contineretur et inserta esset tota oratio dominicalis, videlicet Pater Noster, etc., et tota series presentis testamentj. Et taliter me, Petrum, notarium infrascriptum, rogavit ut de predictis publicum conficerem instrumentum.

6. April 27, 1481. Agreement between Angelica di Leonardo Malefici, the widow of Guasparre dal Lama, and the monastery of Santa Maria Novella for the endowment of the Cappella de' Magi (ASF, Notarile Antecosimiano, P 353 [Ser Piero da Vinci, 1478-81], fols. 599v-600v):

Item postea dictis anno, jndictione et dicta die xxvij dicti mensis Aprilis. Actum Florentie in populo sanctj Paulj in domo habitationis infrascripte domine Angelice, presentibus testibus, etc.: Niccholao Jacobj Charduccj et Johanne Bastianj Ormannj et Pulinario Phylippj Simonis Salamonis del Garbo aromatorio, civibus Florentinis.

Mundualdus:

Domina Angelica vidua, filia olim Leonardj Luce Maleficj et uxor olim et ultimo Guasparis Zenobij de Lama, sensalis cambiorum, populj sancti Paulj de Florentia, constituta in presentia mej, notarij infrascripti, etc., dixit se proprio mundualdo carere, cuius consensu possit et valeat se obligare, etc.; et propterea petijt in eius mundualdum, etc., Angelum Mariam, eius fratrem carnalem et filium dictj olim Leonardj Luce Malefici, ibidem presentem et volentem, etc.; quem dedj, etc., interponens, etc.; rogans, etc.

Convenctio:

Item postea ibidem jncontinentj, eisdem anno, jndictione et die et loco, et coram dictis suprascriptis testibus, etc.

Prefata domina Angelicha, cum consensu, verbo, licentia et auctoritate dictj Angelj Marie, eius fratris carnalis et legiptimj mundualdj predictj, ibidem presentis et eidem consentientis, etc.; et certificata primo et ante omnia de iuribus suis et de vj et inportantia presentis contractus et de benefitio velleanj, etc., de quibus omnibus dixit se plenissime jnformatam, etc.; considerans qualiter de intentione et voluntate dictj Guasparis, olim suj virj et maritj predefuntj, fuit et erat dotare quandam cappellam per ipsum olim Guasparem constructam et edificatam jn ecclesia sanctae Marie Novelle de Florentia, ordinis Predicatorum, sub titulo sanctorum Maghorum, de redditu et proventu quolibet anno jn perpetuum librarum quinquaginta soldorum parvorum; et attento qualiter postea dictus Guaspar per suum ultimum testamentum et ultimam voluntatem super hoc nullam fecit provisionem nec ordinationem; credens talem ordinationem fecisse per quandam donationem causa mortis per ipsum Guasparrem jamdiu factam, et per dictum suum ultimum testamentum non fore revocatam; que donatio in veritate restabat inanris per dictum suum testamentum, in quo nullam fecit mentionem de dicta donatione—ymo re-

vocavit, capsavit et annullavit quamlibet et quamcumque aliam suam
ultimam voluntatem; in qua revocatione venit etiam dicta donatio
causa mortis, et hoc processit potius ex inadvertentia quam consulte
et advertenter; et considerata benivolentia et amore quem ipse
Guaspar tam in vita quam etiam in morte et eius ultima voluntate
semper habuit et obstendit erga ipsam dominam Angelicam, et quam
ardenter ipsam dilexit, consonum et pium sibj videtur quod id quod
de eius jntentione fuit et erat per eam, iuxta posse, debite executionj
demandare et salubriter anime sue providere; jdcirco, ex eius mera
et libera voluntate, et non coacta neque aliquo modo circumventa,
etc., et omnj modo, etc., promisit et solempnj stipulatione convenit
venerabilj viro magistro Johannj Carolj de Florentia, sacre pagine
profexorj necnon priorj dictj convenctus sancte Marie Novelle de
Florentia, ordinis Predicatorum, ibidem presentj et pro dicto monasterio, capitulo et convenctu recipienti et stipulanti, jnfra sex menses
proxime futuros, omnj exceptione et gavillatione penitus remotjs,
emere et seu emj facere jn civitate et seu comitatu Florentie tot bona
inmobilia de voluntate, presentia, consensu et ad declarationem dictj
prioris, fratruum, capitulj et convenctus sancte Marie Novelle de
Florentia, et pro ipsa cappella sanctorum Magorum, quorum fructus,
redditus et provenctus adscendant ad veram et legiptimam valutam
pro quolibet anno in perpetuum librarum quinquaginta soldorum
parvorum et florenorum trium aurj largorum, seu facere et curare
ita et taliter cum effectu quod infra dictum tempus heredes et seu
hereditas dictj Guasparis, olim suj virj et maritj, ement dicta bona
dictorum redditus et provenctus quolibet anno, ut prefertur. Qua
emptione facta per dictos heredes et hereditatem seu alium eius et
seu eorum nomine, eo casu ipsa domina Angelica jntelligatur esse et
sit libera et absoluta a presentj obligatione et contractu. Quorum
quidem bonorum sic emendorum fructus, redditus et proventus
pertineant et expectent ad ipsum monasterium, capitulum et con-
venctum sancte Marie Novelle cum jnfrascriptis oneribus, gravedini-
bus et condictionibus, videlicet: quod dictj prior, fratres, capitulum
et convenctus sancte Marie Novelle, pro tempore existentes, teneantur
et obligatj sint qualibet die in perpetuum, incipiendo inmediate secuta
emptione dictorum bonorum, dicere et seu dicj facere pro anima
dictorum Guasparris et suorum mortuorum adminus unam missam
planam, exceptis dumtaxat diebus Jovis, Veneris et Sabbatj sanctj;
jtem quolibet anno jn perpetuum ad ipsum altare facere et celebrare
festivitatem sanctorum Magorum jn die eorum festivitatis cum missis
et cera convenientibus, secundum declarationem prioris, fratruum,
capitulj et convenctus, pro tempore existentis eiusdem convenctus;
jtem ad ipsum altare quolibet anno in perpetuum facere et celebrare, et
seu fierj et celebrarj facere, unum offitium mortuorum pro anima

dictj Guasparis et suorum mortuorum, in die qua dictus Guaspar decessit seu saltem jnfra tres dies inmediate sequentes diem mortis dictj Guasparis, cum cera et missis convenientibus, secundum declarationem predictam; jtem quod continuo teneantur retinere unam lampadam accensam ad ipsum altare. Jn quibus quidem festo sanctorum Magorum et annualj, et lampade [*sic*], adminus expendantur dictj tres florenj largi quolibet anno. Jncipiendo predicta omnia inmediate facta dicta emptione dictorum bonorum, sub onere conscientie dictorum prioris, fratruum, capitulj et convenctus, pro tempore existentium. Et ad sic faciendum et observandum prefatj prior, fratres, capitulum et convenctus teneantur se obligare jn forma juris valida; non propterea preiudicando dicto monasterio, capitulo et convenctuj jn aliquo alio eorum jure; si quo modo reperiretur utilius fuisse dispositum per dictum olim Guasparem, olim virum et maritum dicte domine Angelice, jn aliqua sua ultima voluntate, et talis ultima voluntas esset valida, et eo casu quo melius et utilius reperiretur esse dispositum et ordinatum per dictum Guasparem jn utilitatem dicte cappelle, eo casu stetur et starj debeat talj disposito, et bona ut supra emenda et seu empta cedant pro parte satisfactionis talis dispositi et ordinati. Que omnia prefata domina Angelica promisit, etc. . . .

1. 1617 (1729). Gaetano Martini, *Sepolcrario della chiesa di Santa Maria Novella di Firenze copiato diligentemente dall'originale che è appresso i padri della medesima chiesa* (Ricc., 1935), 1729, fols. 68v-69r:

Altare de' Vecchietti:

Fra due Porte, cioé fra la Porta del Mezzo e la Porta verso S. Benedetto, Altare della Nunziata della famiglia de' Vecchietti, il quale anticamente fu eretto da Giovanni Lami Cittadino Fiorentino insieme con un Sepolcro di Marmo sotto il Titolo dell'Epifania, e chiamavasi "l'Altare de' Magi" perché era stata dipinta nell'Ancona da Sandro Botticelli Pittore eccellentissimo la Storia de' tre Magi, opera maravigliosa tenuta da tutti, la quale in rifare detto Altare fu da Fabio Mandragoni Spagnolo levata e messa nel suo Palazo, che poco lontano dalla detta Chiesa haveva fabbricato, et in quello Scambio vi fece fare quella che di presente si vede, dove da Santi di Tito Pittore rarissimo fu dentrovi dipinto la Vergine annunziata dall'Angelo. Questo Altare fu la prima volta fatto di richissimi Marmi e nobilissimi Intagli ornato dal soprascritto Lami; il quale dopo pervenne nella famiglia dei Fedini. Costoro, dopo haverlo tenuto molti anni, lo venderono a Fabio Mandragoni, che poi rifece l'Altare, guastando il Vecchio per seguitare l'ordine delli Altri, ricoprendo con gli Scalini dell'Altare la sepoltura del primo fondatore di Casa Lami, per farci dinanzi la sua, conforme a che havevano fatto gli altri Padroni delli Altari, i quali in raccomodare la Chiesa posono i loro sepolcri dinanzi ai loro Altari; la qual cosa non seguì perché la cagion non so, e lo vendè a Bernardo di Giovanni Vecchietti con patto di levar l'Arme di Casa sua et invece di quella lasciarci porre quella de' Vecchietti, come al presente vediamo.

[*Below at left*: "La sopradetta Tavola (*scil.*, the *Annunciation* by Santi di Tito) fu fatta fare dai Vecchietti quando finirono del tutto la detta Cappella lasciata imperfetta dal Mandragoni." *Below in center*: the arms of Guasparre dal Lama, a red chevron on a gold or yellow field, with (*above*), "Lamio"; (*below*), "del Lama."]

2. 1617 (1729, 1748). Fra Domenico Sandrini, *Notizie della Chiesa e Convento di Santa Maria Novella . . . raccolte l'anno 1617 da Fra Niccolò Sermartelli Fiorentino Priore del Convento, ricopiate da me da una Copia statane fatta l'anno 1729 dal reveren-*

dissimo Padre Gaetano Martini Fiorentino . . . (BNC, Baldovinetti, 124), 1748 [no foliation]:

   L'Altare che segue dall'altra parte in mezzo alle due Porte prin-
cipali della Chiesa fu eretto in onore de' 3 Re magi da Giovanni del
Lama Cittadino Fiorentino, che vi fece dipingere la Tavola da Sandro
Botticellj Fiorentino, la quale fu reputata una dell'Opere tra le più
eccellenti di quest'Artefice [*in margin*: Avendo Ne' Volti de' Regi
Ritratti 3 Personaggi della Casa Medici come scrive il Baldinucci nel
Tomo terzo all'anno 1470], et era tutto dj marmj intagliati, a piè
di cuj fu egli sepolto con Arme e Lettere che dicevano, "Sep: Guaspar Zenobij de Lama." Ne pervenne dj poi il Padronato ne' Fedinj,
da' quali fu ceduto a Fabio Alzarola Spagnolo marchese di mandra-
gone, Gentiluomo intimo favorito dj Francesco I de' Medici Gran
Duca di Toscana, che abitava la Casa de' Cinj, detta oggi del Mondragone. Questo fecevj erigere l'Altare di Pietramj coll'ordine dellj
altrj, portandosi nel suo vicino Palazzo la tavola del Botticello. Di
poi, caduto in disgrazia del suo Padrone, per la qual convenneli
partire da questo Stato, ne concesse il Padronato a Bernardo dj Giovanni Vecchiettj, che vj pose l'Arme sua, facendovj ancora colorir
la Tavola che vj è dj nostra Signora Annunziata da Santi di Tito
celebre Pittore dal Borgo San Sepolcro, e trasferire a' piedi di esso
l'Antico Lastrone sepolcrale di sua famiglia che già stava nella Croci-
ata destra della Chiesa, in cui si legge inciso: "Sep. nobilium militum
D. Rinuċcinj et D. Gherardi de Vecchiettis, et suorum."

3. 1657 (18th century). Stefano Rosselli, *Sepoltuario Fiorentino
ovvero Descrizione delle Chiese, Cappelle e Sepolture, loro Armi
et Iscrizioni della Città di Firenze e suoi Contorni* (BNC, II, 1,
126), [1657], II, ii, fols. 33v-34r:

No. 621 [Santa Maria Novella]. Entrando in Chiesa per la porta
principale, a mano dritta si trova la Cappella della famiglia de' Vecchietti, intorno alla quale ho da soggiugnere l'appiè notizie: Questa
Cappella fu anticamente eretta da Guasparri Lami Cittadino Fiorentino, e fattavi la sua Sepoltura, che hoggi resta coperta da gli Scalinj
della medesima Cappella. Chiamavasi "la Cappella de' Magi" per una
bella Tavola, nella quale da Sandro Botticelli Pittor raro et eccellente
era stata dipinta quella Storia. Passò non so come questa Cappella
nella famiglia de' Fedini, dalla quale fu venduta a Fabio Mondragone
Spagnuolo, il quale, riducendola nello Stato che al presente si vede, e
pigliando per sé la detta Tavola de' Magi di Sandro Botticelli, vi

fece far da Santi di Tito quella della santissima Nunziata. Fu di poi
la detta Cappella dal Mondragone venduto al Senatore Bernardo Vecchietti, che la fece del tutto; e dal Senatore Filippo, che ancor vive,
fu levata di consenso di tutta la sua famiglia la sepoltura che era nella
Croce della Chiesa accanto a quella della famiglia del Vigna, contras-
segnata del numero 71, e traportata appiè di questa Cappella, e nel
luogo dov'era prima, posto un tavello di marmo di mezzo braccio in
circa, entrovi scolpita la lettera "V;" il medesimo senatore Filippo
Vecchiettj l'anno 1652 fece porre fra il canto e la porta più vicina
a questa Cappella una bella Inscrizione in marmo di Fra Bernardo
Vecchietti Cavaliere Hierosolimitano.

Bibliography

Albertini, Francesco. *Memoriale di molte statue et picture sono nella inclyta ciptà di Florentia.* Ed. Herbert P. Horne. Florence, 1909.

Allegrini, Joseph. *Serie di ritratti d'uomini illustri toscani con gli elogi istorici de' medesimi.* 4 vols. Florence, 1766-73.

Alpers, Svetlana L. "Ekphrasis and Aesthetic Attitudes in Vasari's Lives," *Journal of the Warburg and Courtauld Institutes*, xxiii, 1960, pp. 190-215.

D'Ancona, Alessandro. *Origini del teatro italiano.* 2nd ed. 2 vols. Turin, 1891.

Anonimo Magliabechiano (Gaddiano): see *Il Codice magliabechiano*; and Fabriczy.

Antoninus, Saint, Archbishop of Florence. *Divi Antonini Archiepiscopi Florentini . . . Chronicorum opus.* 3 vols. Lyon, 1587.

———. *Summa theologica.* 4 vols. Graz, 1959.

Anz, Heinrich. *Die lateinischen Magierspiele.* Leipzig, 1905.

Arlotto [Mainardi], Piovano. *Motti e facezie del piovano Arlotto.* Ed. Gianfranco Folena. Milan, 1953.

Arndt, Karl. *Rogier van der Weyden, Der Columba-Altar.* Stuttgart, 1962.

Baldini, Umberto, and Dal Poggetto, Paolo. *Firenze restaura* (catalogue of the exhibition at the Fortezza da Basso, 18 March–4 June 1972). Florence, 1972.

Baldinucci, Filippo. *Notizie de' professori del disegno.* 6 vols. Florence, 1681-1728.

Baldovinetti: see Poggi.

Bandini, Angelo Maria. *Catalogus codicum Latinorum Bibliothecae Mediceae Laurentianae.* 4 vols. Florence, 1774-77.

———. *Specimen literaturae Florentinae saeculi XV. . . . .* 2 vols. Florence, 1748.

Baron, Hans. *The Crisis of the Early Italian Renaissance.* 2 vols. Princeton, 1955.

Baxandall, Michael. *Painting and Experience in Fifteenth Century Italy.* Oxford, 1972.

Beenken, Hermann. *Rogier van der Weyden.* Munich, 1951.

Below, Irene. *Leonardo da Vinci und Filippino Lippi. Studien zu den Altartafeln für die Bernhardskapelle im Palazzo Vecchio und für das Kloster San Donato a Scopeto* (diss. Berlin). Berlin, 1971.

Berenson, Bernard. *Italian Pictures of the Renaissance, Florentine School.* 2 vols. London, 1963.

———. "Postscript, 1949: The Cook Tondo Revisited," in *Homeless Paintings of the Renaissance,* ed. Hanna Kiel, London, 1969, pp. 235-42.

Berlendis, Francisco de. *De oblationibus ad altare.* Venice, 1743.

Bernard of Clairvaux, Saint, Abbot. *Sermones de tempore.* In Migne, *Patrologia Latina,* CLXXXIII, cols. 35-360.

Bettini, Sergio. *Botticelli.* Bergamo, 1942.

Bode, Wilhelm. *Botticelli.* Berlin, 1921.

Borghigiani, Vincenzo. *Cronaca annalistica del convento di Santa Maria Novella* [18th century, Florence, Archivio di Santa Maria Novella], III, pp. 330-40 (based on a description of 1556 of the interior of the church), in Stefano Orlandi, *Necrologio di Santa Maria Novella,* Florence, 1955, II, pp. 397-404.

Borghini, Raffaello. *Il Riposo.* Florence, 1584.

Borsook, Eve. *The Companion Guide to Florence.* London, 1966.

Braun, Joseph. *Die liturgische Gewandung im Occident und Orient.* Freiburg, 1907.

———. *Die liturgischen Paramente in Gegenwart und Vergangenheit.* 2nd ed. Freiburg, 1924.

Brockhaus, Heinrich. *Forschungen über Florentiner Kunstwerke.* Leipzig, 1902.

Brockwell, Maurice. *The "Adoration of the Magi" by Jan Mabuse.* London, 1911.

Browe, Peter. *Die Verehrung der Eucharistie im Mittelalter.* Munich, 1933.

Brown, Alison M. "The Humanist Portrait of Cosimo de' Medici, Pater Patriae," *Journal of the Warburg and Courtauld Institutes,* xxiv, 1961, pp. 186-221.

Brown, James Wood. *The Dominican Church of Santa Maria Novella at Florence.* Edinburgh, 1902.

Buser, Benjamin. *Die Beziehungen der Mediceer zu Frankreich während der Jahre 1434-1494.* Leipzig, 1879.

Catalago della Mostra d'Arte Antica: Lorenzo il Magnifico e le arti. Florence, 1949.

Chastel, André. *Art et humanisme à Florence au temps de Laurent le Magnifique.* Paris, 1959.

———. *Marsil Ficin et l'art.* Geneva, 1954.

Chrysostom, John, Saint. *De incomprehensibili Dei natura, etc., homiliae xii*. In Migne, *Patrologia Graeca*, XLVIII, cols. 701-812.

———. *Homilies on First Corinthians*. In *A Select Library of the Nicene and Post-Nicene Fathers of the Christian Church*. Ed. Philip Schaff. New York, 1889, XII, pp. 1-269.

Clark, Kenneth. *Leonardo da Vinci*. New York, 1939.

Il Codice magliabechiano contentente notizie . . . scritte da anonimo fiorentino. Ed. Carl Frey. Berlin, 1892.

Corella, Domenico da. *Theotocon*, III-IV, in *Deliciae eruditorum*, ed. Giovanni Lami, Florence, 1742, XII (XIII), pp. 49-116.

Cornell, Henrik. *The Iconography of the Nativity of Christ* (Uppsala Universitets Årsskrift, 1924, 1). Uppsala, 1924.

Covi, Dario. "Botticelli and Pope Sixtus IV," *Burlington Magazine*, cxi, 1969, pp. 616f.

Creizenach, Wilhelm. *Geschichte des neueren Dramas*. 5 vols. Halle, 1893-1916.

Crombach, Heinrich. *Primitiae gentium, seu historiae ss. trium Magorum evangelicorum, et encomium*. Cologne, 1654.

Davies, Martin. *The Earlier Italian Schools* (National Gallery Catalogues). London, 1961.

Dix, Gregory. *The Shape of the Liturgy*. London, 1945.

Doren, Alfred. *Studien aus der Florentiner Wirtschaftsgeschichte*. 2 vols. Stuttgart, 1901-8.

Doria, Gino. *Il Museo e la Certosa di S. Martino*. Naples, 1964.

Dumoutet, Edouard. *Le Désir de voir l'hostie*. Paris, 1926.

Durandus, Guglielmus. *Rationale divinorum officiorum*. Naples, 1859.

———. *Speculum iuris*. 4 vols. Venice, 1576.

Eisler, Colin. "The Athlete of Virtue: The Iconography of Asceticism," in *De artibus opuscula XL: Essays in Honor of Erwin Panofsky*, ed. Millard Meiss, New York, 1961, pp. 82-97.

Fabriczy, Cornelius von. "Il Codice dell'Anonimo Gaddiano (Cod. Magliabechiano XVII, 17) nella Biblioteca Nazionale di Firenze," *Archivio storico italiano*, series v, xii, 1893, II, pp. 15-94.

Fiamma, Galvano. *De rebus gestis . . . a Vicecomitibus*. In *Rerum Italicorum scriptores*. Ed. Ludovico Antonio Muratori, Milan, 1728, XII, cols. 997-1050.

Ficino, Marsilio. *Opera omnia*. 2 vols. Basle, 1576 (Turin, 1959).

Fineschi, Vincenzo. *Della festa e della processione del Corpus Domini in Firenze*. Florence, 1768.

A Florentine Picture-Chronicle . . . by Maso Finiguerra. Ed. Sidney Colvin. London, 1898.

Formularium modernum et universale diversorum contractuum nuper emendatum per eximium legum Doctorem Florentinum Dominum

Leonardum de Colle . . . [Florence, Bartolommeo de' Libri, after 15 December 1488].

Forsyth, Ilene Haering. "Magi and Majesty: A Study of Romanesque Sculpture and Liturgical Drama," *Art Bulletin*, l, 1968, pp. 215-22.

Francesco di Giorgio Martini. *Trattati di architettura, ingegneria e arte militare.* Ed. Corrado Maltese. 2 vols. Milan, 1967.

Freedberg, Sydney J. *Painting of the High Renaissance in Rome and Florence.* 2 vols. Cambridge, Mass., 1961.

Gilbert, Creighton. Review of John Pope-Hennessy, *The Portrait in the Renaissance, Burlington Magazine*, cx, 1968, pp. 278-85.

Gombrich, Ernst H. "The Early Medici as Patrons of Art: A Survey of Primary Sources," in *Norm and Form: Studies in the Art of the Renaissance*, London, 1966, pp. 35-57.

Hartt, Frederick. *History of Italian Renaissance Art.* New York, 1969.

Hatfield, Rab. "The Compagnia de' Magi," *Journal of the Warburg and Courtauld Institutes*, xxxiii, 1970, pp. 107-61.

——. "Five Early Renaissance Portraits," *Art Bulletin*, xlvii, 1965, pp. 315-34.

——. "Some Unknown Descriptions of the Medici Palace in 1459," *Art Bulletin*, lii, 1970, pp. 232-49.

Hatfield Strens, Bianca. "L'arrivo del trittico Portinari a Firenze," *Commentari*, xix, 1968, pp. 315-19.

Heydenreich, Ludwig H. *Leonardo da Vinci.* 2 vols. New York, 1954.

Hill, George F. *A Corpus of Italian Medals of the Renaissance before Cellini.* 2 vols. London, 1930.

Horne, Herbert P. *Alessandro Filipepi Commonly Called Sandro Botticelli.* London, 1908.

——. "The Story of a Famous Botticelli," *Monthly Review*, vi, 2, no. 17, February 1902, pp. 133-44.

Innocent III, Pope. *Sermones de sanctis.* In Migne, *Patrologia Latina*, ccxvii, cols. 451-596.

Jungmann, Josef A. *The Mass of the Roman Rite: Its Origins and Development (Missarum Sollemnia).* Trans. Frederick A. Brunner. 2 vols. New York, 1950.

Kehrer, Hugo. *Die heiligen drei Könige in Literatur und Kunst.* 2 vols. Leipzig, 1908-9.

Kiesow, Gottfried. "Die gotische Südfassade von S. Maria Novella in Florenz," *Zeitschrift für Kunstgeschichte*, xxv, 1962, pp. 1-12.

King, Archdale A. *Liturgies of the Primatial Sees.* London, 1957.

——. *Notes on the Catholic Liturgies.* London, 1930.

Kristeller, Paul Oskar. *The Philosophy of Marsilio Ficino.* New York, 1943.

Langedijk, Karla. *De portretten van de Medici tot omstreeks 1600* (diss. Amsterdam). Assen, 1968.

Lavin, Marilyn Aronberg. "Piero della Francesca's Flagellation: The Triumph of Christian Glory," *Art Bulletin*, l, 1968, pp. 321-42.

Leo III, Saint, Pope. *Sermones*. In Migne, *Patrologia Latina*, LIV, cols. 137-468.

Leonardo da Colle: see *Formularium*.

Il Libro di Antonio Billi. Ed. Carl Frey. Berlin, 1892.

Lorenzoni, A. *Cosimo Rosselli*. Florence, 1921.

Marle, Raimond van. *The Development of the Italian Schools of Painting*. 19 vols. The Hague, 1923-38.

Martène, Edmond. *De antiquis Ecclesiae ritibus libri quatuor*. 4 vols. Bassano, 1788.

Meersseman, Gilles. "Etudes sur les anciennes confréries dominicaines, II: Les confréries de Saint Pierre Martyr," *Archivum Fratrum Praedicatorum*, xxi, 1951, pp. 62-66.

Meller, Peter. "La Cappella Brancacci: Problemi ritrattistici ed iconografici," *Acropoli*, i, 1960-61, pp. 186-227, 273-312.

Mesnil, Jacques. *Botticelli*. Paris, 1938.

––––––. "La Compagnia di Gesù Pellegrino," *Rivista d'Arte*, ii, 1904, pp. 64-73.

––––––. "L'Influence flamande chez Domenico Ghirlandaio," *La Revue de l'art ancien et moderne*, xxix, 1911, pp. 61-76.

––––––. "Quelques documents sur Botticelli," *Miscellanea d'arte*, i, 1903, pp. 80-98.

––––––. "Sigismondo Malatesta e Galeazzo Maria Sforza in un affresco del Gozzoli," *Rassegna d'arte*, ix, 1909, pp. 74f.

Möller, Emil. "Leonardos Bildnis der Cecilia Gallerani in der Galerie des Fürsten Czartoryski in Krakau," *Monatshefte für Kunstwissenschaft*, ix, 1916, pp. 313-26.

Morçay, Raoul. "La cronaca del convento fiorentino di San Marco," *Archivio storico italiano*, lxxi, 1913, pp. 1-29.

Morelli, Giovanni and Lionardo. *Chroniche*. In *Delizie degli eruditi toscani*. Ed. Ildefonso di San Luigi. Florences, 1785, xix.

Müller-Walde, Paul. *Leonardo da Vinci*. Munich, 1889.

Müntz, Eugène. *Les Collections des Médicis au quinzième siècle*. Paris, 1888.

Nesi, Giovanni. *Iohannes Nesii Oratio de charitate*. . . . Florence: Ser Francesco de' Buonaccorsi [c. 1486].

Nilgen, Ursula. "The Epiphany and the Eucharist: On the Interpretoscani. Ed. Ildefonso di San Luigi. Florence, 1785, xix. *Bulletin*, xlix, 1967, pp. 311-16.

Orlandi, Stefano. *Necrologio di Santa Maria Novella*. 2 vols. Florence, 1955.

Paatz, Walter and Elizabeth. *Die Kirchen von Florenz*. 6 vols. Frankfort, 1940-54.

Palude, Petrus de. *Sermones Thesauri novi de sanctis*. Nuremberg: Anton Koberger, 1487.

———. *Sermones Thesauri novi de tempore*. Nuremberg: Anton Koberger, 1487.

Panofsky, Erwin. *Early Netherlandish Painting*. 2 vols. Cambridge, Mass., 1953.

Passavant, Günther. *Verrocchio*. London, 1969.

Peebles, Ruth J. "The Dry Tree: Symbol of Death," in *Vassar Medieval Studies*, ed. Christabel F. Fiske, New Haven, 1923, pp. 59-79.

Philip, Lotte Brand. "The Prado Epiphany by Jerome Bosch," *Art Bulletin*, xxxv, 1953, pp. 267-93.

Pieraccini, Gaetano. *La stirpe de' Medici di Cafaggiolo*. 3 vols. Florence, 1924.

Pittaluga, Mary. *Filippo Lippi*. Florence, 1949.

Poggi, Giovanni. "La Giostra Medicea del 1475 e la 'Pallade' del Botticelli," *L'Arte*, v, 1902, pp. 71-77.

———. *I Ricordi di Alesso Baldovinetti, nuovamente pubblicati e illustrati*. Florence, 1909.

Poliziano, Angelo. *Congiura de' Pazzi*. Ed. Anicio Bonucci. Florence, 1895.

———. *Della congiura dei Pazzi (Coniurationis commentarium)*. Ed. Alessandro Perosa. Padua, 1958.

———. *Stanze cominciate per la giostra di Giuliano de' Medici*. Ed. Vincenzo Pernicone. Turin, 1954.

Pope-Hennessy, John. *Fra Angelico*. London, 1952.

———. *The Portrait in the Renaissance*. New York, 1966.

Procacci, Ugo. "L'uso dei documenti negli studi di storia dell'arte e le vicende politiche ed economiche in Firenze durante il primo Quattrocento nel loro rapporto con gli artisti," in *Donatello e il suo tempo: Atti dell'VIII Convegno internazionale di studi sul Rinascimento*, Florence, 1968, pp. 11-39.

Pudelko, Georg. "Studien über Domenico Veneziano," *Mitteilungen des kunsthistorischen Instituts in Florenz*, iv, 1932-34, pp. 145-200.

Réau, Louis. *Iconographie de l'art chrétien*. 3 vols. Paris, 1955-59.

Richa, Giuseppe. *Notizie istoriche delle chiese fiorentine*. 10 vols. Florence, 1754-62.

Ring, Grete. *A Century of French Painting, 1400-1500*. London, 1949.

Rochon, André. *La Jeunesse de Laurent de Médicis (1449-1478)*. Paris, 1963.

Salvemini, Gaetano. *La dignità cavalleresca nel comune di Firenze*. Florence, 1896.

Salvini, Roberto. *Tutta la pittura del Botticelli*. 2 vols. Milan, 1958.

Saxl, Friedrich. "The Classical Inscription in Renaissance Art and Politics," *Journal of the Warburg and Courtauld Institutes*, iv, 1941, pp. 19-46.

Schaeffer, Emil. "Ein Medicäer-Bildnis von Mantegna," *Monatshefte für Kunstwissenschaft*, v, 1912, pp. 17-21.

Scharf, Alfred. *Filippino Lippi*. Vienna, 1935.

Schiller, Gertrud. *Ikonographie der christlichen Kunst*. Gütersloh, 1966-.

Schottmüller, Frida. *Fra Angelico da Fiesole, Des Meisters Gemälde*. Stuttgart, 1911.

Stange, Alfred. *Die deutschen Tafelbilder vor Dürer*. Munich, 1967-.

Steinmann, Ernst. *Die sixtinische Kapelle*. 3 vols. Munich, 1901-5.

Storia di Milano. 16 vols. Milan: Fondazione Treccani degli Alfieri, 1953-62.

Sturdevant, Winifred. *The Misterio de los Reyes Magos: Its Position in the Development of the Medieval Legend of the Three Kings* (Johns Hopkins Studies in Romance Literature and Languages, x). Baltimore, 1927.

Thiers, Jean-Baptiste. *Traitez des cloches et de la sainteté de l'offrande du pain et du vin aux messes des morts*. Paris, 1721.

Trapesnikoff, Trifon. *Die Porträtdarstellungen der Mediceer des XV. Jahrhunderts*. Strasburg, 1909.

Ulmann, Heinrich. *Sandro Botticelli*. Munich, 1893.

Varagine, Jacobus de. *Legenda Aurea*. Ed. Theodor Graesse. Dresden, 1846.

———. *Sermones de sanctis*. Lyon: Martin Boillon [c. 1500].

———. *Sermones de tempore*. Lyon: Martin Boillon [c. 1500].

Vasari, Giorgio. *Le vite de' più eccellenti architetti, pittori et scultori italiani*. 2 vols. Florence, 1550.

———. *Le vite de' più eccellenti pittori, scultori e architetti*. 14 vols. Florence: Felice Le Monnier, 1846-70.

———. *Le vite de' più eccellenti pittori, scultori ed architettori*. In *Opere*. Ed. Gaetano Milanesi. 9 vols. Florence, 1878-85.

———. *Lo zibaldone*. Ed. Alessandro del Vita. Rome, 1938.

Venturi, Adolfo. *Storia dell' arte italiana*. 11 vols. Milan, 1901-39.

Vespasiano da Bisticci. *Vite di uomini illustri del secolo XV*. Ed. Paolo d'Ancona and Eberhard Aeschlimann. Milan, 1951.

La vita del beato Ieronimo Savonarola scritta da un anonimo del secolo XVI e già attribuita a fra Pacifico Burlamacchi. Ed. Piero Ginori Conti. Florence, 1937.

Warburg, Aby. *Gesammelte Schriften*. 2 vols. Leipzig, 1932.

Yashiro, Yukio. *Sandro Botticelli*. 3 vols. London, 1925.

Young, Karl. *The Drama of the Medieval Church*. 2 vols. Oxford, 1933.

Index

[141]

Illustrations

1. Sandro Botticelli, *Adoration of the Magi*. Florence, Uffizi

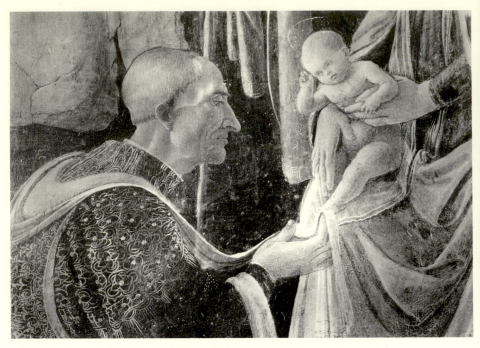

2. Botticelli, *Adoration of the Magi* (detail: old Magus and Christ). Uffizi

3. Botticelli, *Adoration of the Magi* (detail: central
Magus [Piero de' Medici?]). Uffizi

4. Botticelli, *Adoration of the Magi* (detail: bystanders and wall at right). Uffizi

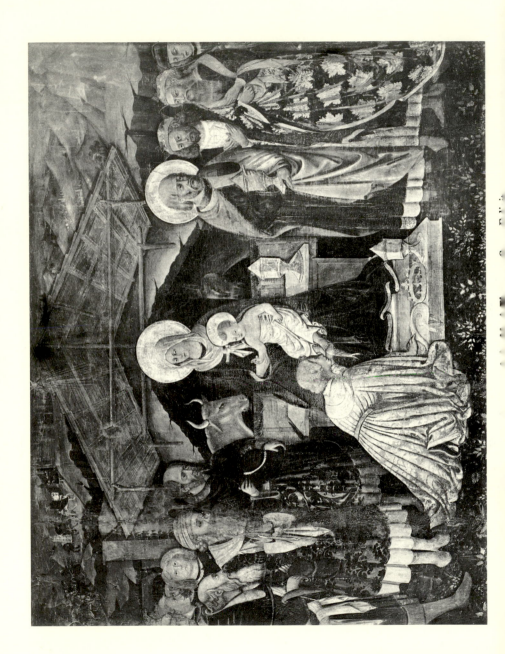

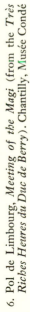

7. Pol de Limbourg, *Adoration of the Magi* (from the *Très Riches Heures du Duc de Berry*). Chantilly, Musée Condé

6. Pol de Limbourg, *Meeting of the Magi* (from the *Très Riches Heures du Duc de Berry*). Chantilly, Musée Condé

8. Sandro Botticelli, *Madonna of the Eucharist*. Boston, Isabella Stewart Gardner Museum

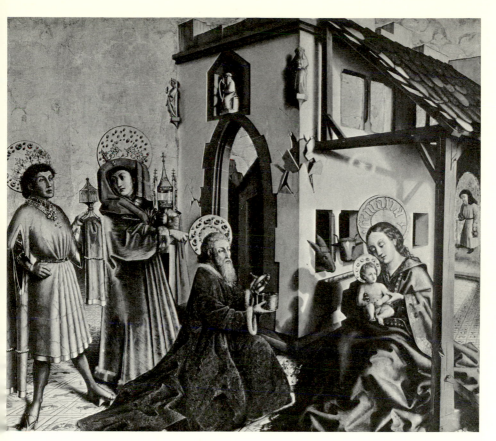

9. Conrad Witz, *Adoration of the Magi*, 1444. Geneva, Musée d'Art et d'Histoire

Gentile da Fabriano, *Adoration of the Magi,* 1423, Florence, Uffizi

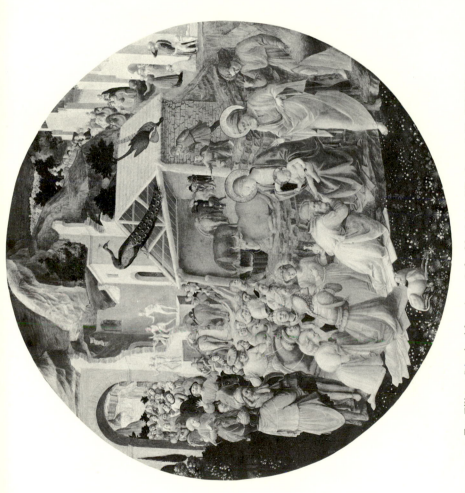

11. Fra Filippo Lippi, *Adoration of the Magi* (the "Cook tondo"). Washington, National Gallery of Art, Samuel H. Kress Collection

12. Sandro Botticelli, *Adoration of the Magi*. London, National Gallery

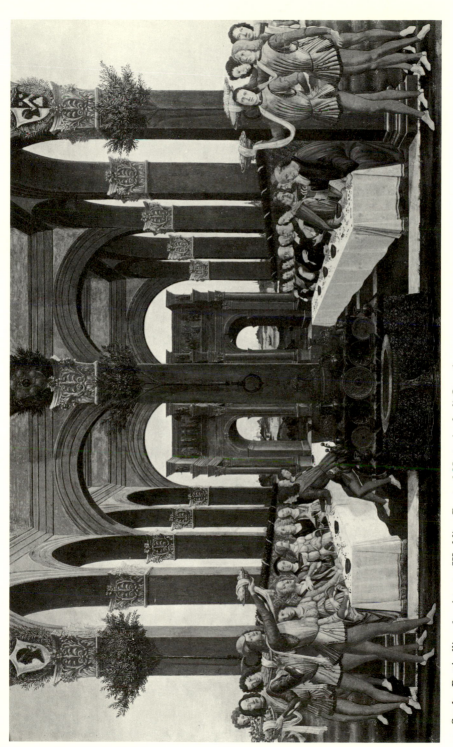

13. Sandro Botticelli and assistants, *Wedding Feast of Nastagio degli Onesti*

14. Sandro Botticelli, *Adoration of the Magi*. London, National Gallery

15. Botticelli, *Adoration of the Magi* (detail: bystanders at left). London

16. Botticelli, *Adoration of the Magi* (detail: young Magus). Uffizi

17. Agnolo Bronzino, *Giovanni de'
Medici*. Florence, Museo Mediceo

18. Giorgio Vasari, *Giovanni de' Medici*. Florence,
Palazzo Vecchio, Sala di Cosimo il Vecchio

19. Botticelli, *Adoration of the Magi* (detail: figure in group of bystanders at left). Uffizi

20. Agnolo Bronzino, *Lorenzo di Giovanni de' Medici*. Florence, Museo
Mediceo

21. Giorgio Vasari, *Lorenzo di Giovanni de' Medici*. Florence,
Palazzo Vecchio, Sala di Cosimo il Vecchio

22. Benozzo Gozzoli, *Voyage of the Magi* (detail: young Magus). Palazzo Medici-Riccardi

23. Benozzo Gozzoli, *Voyage of the Magi* (detail: followers of the young Magus). Palazzo Medici-Riccardi

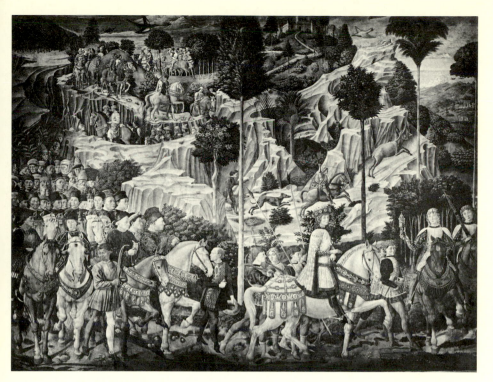

24. Benozzo Gozzoli, *Voyage of the Magi* (detail: right-hand wall), 1459. Florence, Palazzo Medici-Riccardi, Chapel

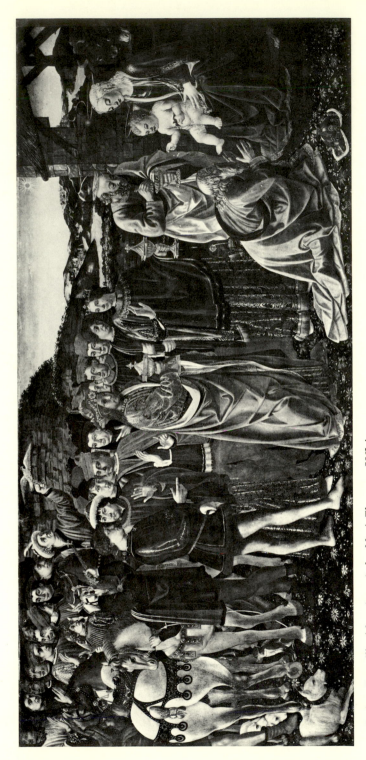

25. Cosimo Rosselli, *Adoration of the Magi*. Florence, Uffizi

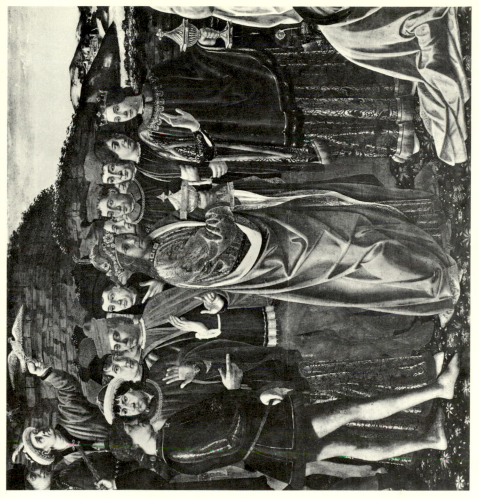

26. Cosimo Rosselli, *Adoration of the Magi* (detail: central group). Uffizi.

28. Sandro Botticelli, *Portrait of a Man Holding a Medal of Cosimo de' Medici*, Florence, Uffizi

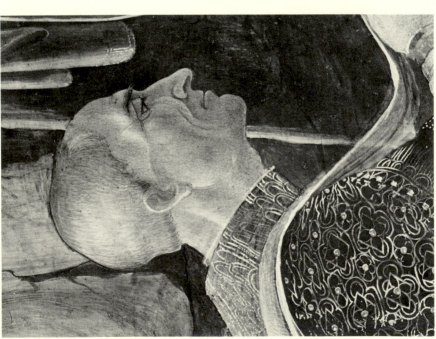

27. Botticelli, *Adoration of the Magi* (detail: old Magus [Cosimo de' Medici]), Uffizi

30. *Medal of Cosimo de' Medici* (Hill, no. 910)

29. *Medal of Cosimo de' Medici* (Hill, no. 909)

32. Piero Pollaiuolo, *Portrait of Galeazzo Maria Sforza* (?). Florence, Uffizi

31. Botticelli, *Adoration of the Magi* (detail: youth with sword [Giuliano de' Medici?]). Uffizi

33. Sandro Botticelli, *Posthumous Portrait of Giuliano de' Medici*. Washington, National Gallery of Art, Samuel H. Kress Collection

34. Andrea del Verrocchio, *Bust of Giuliano de' Medici*. Washington, National Gallery of Art, Andrew Mellon Collection

35. Bertoldo di Giovanni, *Medal of the Pazzi Conspiracy*
(Hill, no. 915): Lorenzo de' Medici

36. Bertoldo di Giovanni, *Medal of the Pazzi Conspiracy*:
Giuliano de' Medici

37. Niccolò Fiorentino, *Medal of Lorenzo de'*
Medici (Hill, no. 926)

38. Agnolo Bronzino, *Giuliano de' Medici.*
Florence, Museo Mediceo

40. Giorgio Vasari, *Giuliano de' Medici*. Florence, Palazzo Vecchio, Sala di Lorenzo il Magnifico

39. Botticelli, *Adoration of the Magi* (detail: erect figure behind Caspar [Lorenzo de' Medici?]). Uffizi

41. Domenico Ghirlandaio, *Confirmation of the Franciscan Rule* (detail: Antonio Pucci, Lorenzo de' Medici, Francesco Sassetti and son), c. 1483. Florence, Santa Trinita, Sassetti Chapel

42. Florentine, 1465-69, *Initial "E" with Alamanno Rinuccini and Lorenzo de' Medici*. Laur., Plut. 65.27, fol. 113v

43. *Medal of Lorenzo de' Medici* (Hill, no. 921)

44. *Medal of Giovanni de' Medici* (Hill, no. 907)

45. Mino da Fiesole, *Bust of a Man* (*Giovanni de' Medici?*).
Florence, Bargello

46. Benozzo Gozzoli, *Voyage of the Magi* (detail: Cosimo [?], Carlo [?], and Piero de' Medici). Palazzo Medici-Riccardi

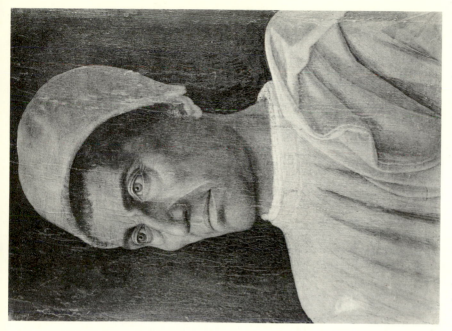

48. Andrea Mantegna, *Portrait of Carlo de' Medici (?)*. Florence, Uffizi

47. Mino da Fiesole, *Bust of Piero de' Medici*, 1453. Florence, Bargello

49. Benozzo Gozzoli, *Voyage of the Magi* (detail: Piero de' Medici). Palazzo Medici-Riccardi

50. *Medal of Piero de' Medici* (Hill, no. 908)

51. Jean Fouquet, *Adoration of the Magi* (from the *Hours of Étienne Chevalier*).
Chantilly, Musée Condé

52. Raphael. *School of Athens*, 1510-11. Rome, Vatican Palace, Stanza della Segnatura

54. Botticelli, *Adoration of the Magi* (detail: self-portrait [?]). Uffizi

53. Botticelli, *Adoration of the Magi* (detail: Guasparre dal Lama). Uffizi

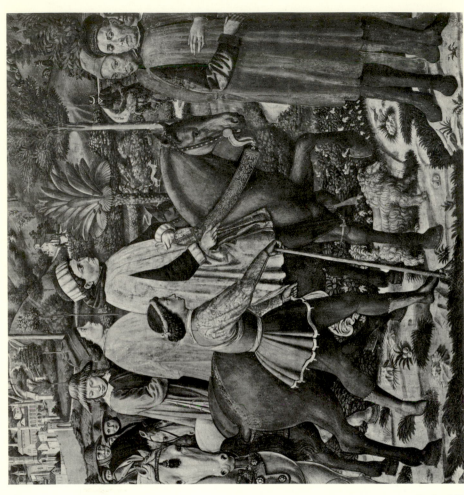

55. Benozzo Gozzoli, *St. Augustine Departing for Milan* (detail: self-portrait), 1465. San Gimignano, Sant'Agostino, Cappella Maggiore

57. Domenico Ghirlandaio, *Expulsion of Joachim from the Temple* (detail: self-portrait), c. 1490. Florence, Santa Maria Novella, Cappella Maggiore

56. Domenico Ghirlandaio, *St. Francis Raising the Spini Child* (detail: self-portrait), c. 1484. Florence, Santa Trinita, Sassetti Chapel

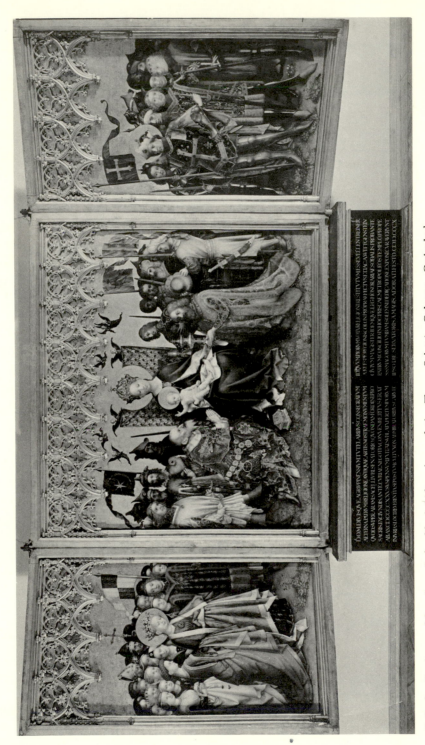

58. Stefan Lochner, *Adoration of the Magi* (Altarpiece of the Town Saints). Cologne, Cathedral

59. Roger van der Weyden, *Adoration of the Magi* (central panel of the Columba Altarpiece). Munich, Alte Pinakothek

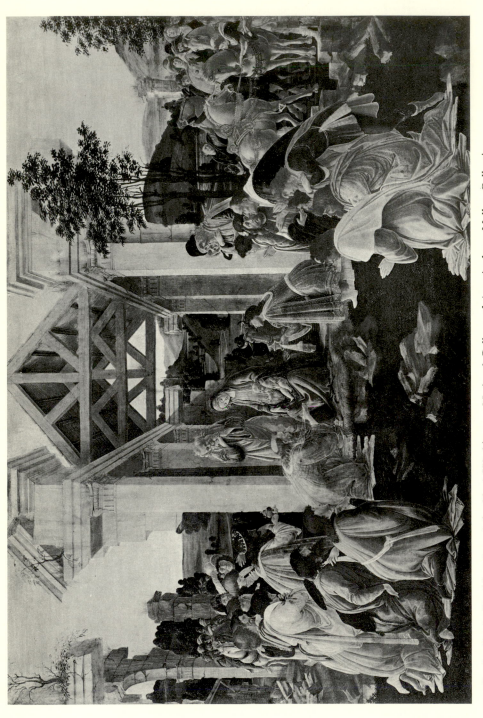

60. Sandro Botticelli, *Adoration of the Magi*. Washington, National Gallery of Art, Andrew Mellon Collection

62. Filippino Lippi, *Adoration of the Magi*, 1496. Florence, Uffizi

61. Domenico Ghirlandaio, *Adoration of the Magi*, 1487.
Florence, Uffizi

63. Leonardo da Vinci, *Adoration of the Magi*, 1481. Florence, Uffizi

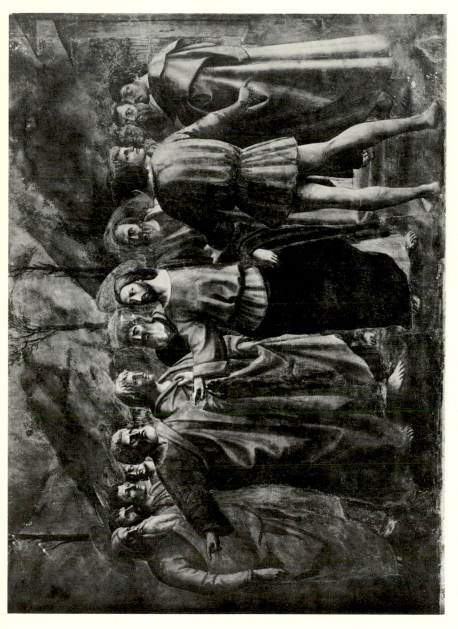

64. Masaccio, *Tribute Money* (detail: *Christ's Command to St. Peter*). Florence, Santa Maria del Carmine, Brancacci Chapel

65. Giotto, *Ascent of St. John the Evangelist into Heaven* (detail: figures at left).
Florence, Santa Croce, Peruzzi Chapel

66. Hugo van der Goes, *Adoration of the Shepherds* (central panel of the Portinari Triptych), c. 1477. Florence, Uffizi

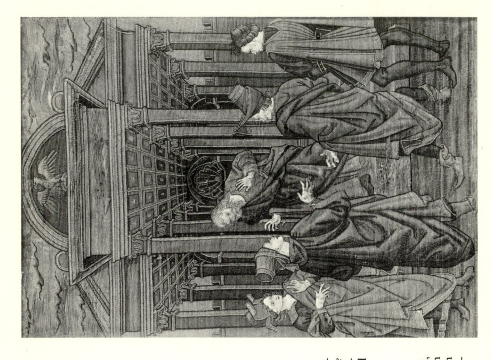

67. Designed by Antonio Pollaiuolo, *Zacharias Leaving the Temple* (embroidery). Florence, Museo dell'Opera del Duomo

68. (*Far right*) Sandro Botticelli, *St. Sebastian*, 1474. Berlin (West), Staatliche Museen Preussischer Kulturbesitz, Gemäldegalerie

Color plate: Sandro Botticelli, *Adoration of the Magi.* Florence, Uffizi